# Nelson Spelling 4

**Clare Kosnik and Donna Duplak**

**Series Authors**

Donna Duplak
Deb Kekewich
Jim Kekewich
Clare Kosnik
Louis Quildon
Edgar Schmidt
Catherine Walker

*Clare Kosnik, Senior Author*

 ITP Nelson

*an International Thompson Publishing company*

Toronto • Albany • Bonn • Boston • Cincinnati • Detroit • London • Madrid • Melbourne
Mexico City • New York • Pacific Grove • Paris • San Francisco • Singapore • Tokyo • Washington

I(T)P® **International Thomson Publishing**
The trademark ITP is used under licence

© I(T)P® **Nelson**
A Division of International Thomson Limited, 1997
All rights in this book are reserved

Published in 1997 by
Nelson Canada,
A Division of International Thomson Limited
1120 Birchmount Road
Scarborough, Ontario
M1K 5G4

ISBN 0-17-604814-6

**Canadian Cataloguing in Publication Data**

Kosnik, Clare
 Nelson Spelling 4

ISBN 0-17-604814-6

1. Spellers.  2. English language - Orthography and spelling - Problems, exercises, etc.  I. Duplak, Donna. II. Title.

PE1145.2.K67 1996      428.1      C96-930591-5

Series Editor: Alan Simpson
Project Editor: Jennifer Rowsell
Series Designer: Peggy Rhodes
Cover Illustrator: Normon Eyolfson
Senior Composition Analyst/Designer: Suzanne Peden
Production: Donna Brown
Permissions: Vicki Gould
Digital Media: Sarah Clarke
Photography: Ray Boudreau

Printed and bound in Canada by Metropole Litho

**Reviewers**
The authors and publishers gratefully acknowledge the contributions of the following educators:

| | | | |
|---|---|---|---|
| Paul D'Agostino<br>Mississauga, Ontario | Dena Domijan<br>Burnaby, British Columbia | Joanne Hull<br>Ajax, Ontario | Lori Rog<br>Regina, Saskatchewan |
| Halina Bartley<br>Peterborough, Ontario | Diane Furry<br>Hannon, Ontario | Joanne LeBlanc-Haley<br>Fredericton, New Brunswick | Bob Shields<br>Wolfville, Nova Scotia |
| Debbie Brandell<br>Edmonton, Alberta | Dr. Georgina Hedges<br>St. John's, Newfoundland | Thea Morris<br>Calgary, Alberta | Gordon Williamson<br>Winnipeg, Manitoba |

4 5 ML 00 99 98

**Acknowledgements**

Permission to reprint copyright material is gratefully acknowledged. Every reasonable effort to trace the copyright holders of materials appearing in this book has been made. Information that will enable the publisher to rectify any error or omission will be welcomed.

"Fast Freddy" by Ann McKay, used by permission of the author; "The Acrobats" by Shel Silverstein, from *Where the Sidewalk Ends*, copyright © 1974 by Evil Eye Music, Inc. Reprinted by permission of HarperCollins Publishers; "A School of Fish" reprinted with permission from *Pride of Lions* by Nicola Morgan, copyright Nicola Morgan, published by Fitzhenry & Whiteside; "Eletelephony" from *Tirra Lirra* by Laura E. Richards. Copyright 1930, 1932 by Laura E. Richards; copyright © renewed 1960 by Hamilton Richards. Reprinted by permission of Little, Brown and Company; "The Apple and the Worm" by Robert Heidbreder, from *Don't Eat Spiders* © 1985 Robert Heidbreder, reprinted by permission of Oxford University Press Canada. Illustration—chum mcleod; The first paragraph of *The Velveteen Rabbit* by Margery Williams is reprinted courtesy of Henry Holt and Company, Inc.

**Illustrators**
The authors and publishers gratefully acknowledge the contributions of the following illustrators: Susanna Denti, Daniel Dumont, John Etheridge, Norman Eyolfson, Franklin Hammond, Jun Park, and Dusan Petricic.

**Photographs**

p. 53 – Andy Sacks / Tony Stone Images
p. 61 – Mary Kate Denny / Tony Stone Images
p. 79 – Lawrence Migdale / Tony Stone Images
p. 91 – Chip Henderson / Tony Stone Images
p. 132 – Arthur Tilley – FPG / Masterfile

# Table of Contents

**Lesson**      **Page**

**1**    **Short Vowel Sounds**
     STRATEGY:    Make a Rhyming Word    8
                 Connecting with Math (Graphing)

**2**    **Long a**
     STRATEGY:    Say It Slowly    12
                 Focus on Language (Sentence Types)

**3**    **Long e**
     STRATEGY:    Does It Look Right?    16
                 Connecting with Literature
                       (The Little Bird and the Bat)

**4**    **Long i**
     STRATEGY:    Look for Silent e    20
                 Connecting with Literature
                       (The Frog and the Ox)

**5**    **Prefix un-**
     STRATEGY:    Study Your Spelling Words    24
                 Focus on Language (Action Words—Verbs)

**6**    **SPELL CHECK (Review, Lessons 1–6)**    28

**7**    **Long o**
     STRATEGY:    List Challenge Words    30
                 Focus on Language (Descriptions)

**8**    **Long u**
     STRATEGY:    Draw Word Pictures    34
                 Connecting with Art (Word Collage)

**9**    **kn-**
     STRATEGY:    Highlight Beginning Sounds    38
                 Connecting with Physical Education
                       (Sports Mobile)

**10**    **sh**
     STRATEGY:    Make a Foldover    42
                 Focus on Language
                       (Word Shortcuts—Contractions)

**11**    **qu**
     STRATEGY:    Proofreading    46
                 Focus on Language (Capital Letters)

| Lesson | | Page |
|---|---|---|

**12**    **SPELL CHECK (Review, Lessons 7–11)**    **50**

**13**    nk
     **STRATEGY:** Highlight Letters That Need Attention    **52**
     Focus on Language (Getting Ideas)

**14**    ck
     **STRATEGY:** Give It a Go!—Leave a Blank    **56**
     Focus on Language
       (Units of Sound—Syllables)

**15**    -tion
     **STRATEGY:** See It—Visualize Words    **60**
     Connecting with Science (Science Poster)

**16**    ch
     **STRATEGY:** Find Related Words—Meaning Patterns    **64**
     Focus on Language
       (Joined Words—Compounds)

**17**    ough and Challenge Words
     **STRATEGY:** Spelling Traps—Study Challenge Words    **68**
     Connecting with Math (Geometry)

**18**    **SPELL CHECK (Review, Lessons 13–17)**    **72**

**19**    Hard and Soft c
     **STRATEGY:** Proofreading—Scan Back!    **74**
     Connecting with Art
       (The Creative Shape of Words)

**20**    igh, eigh
     **STRATEGY:** I Know That Pattern!—Word Families    **78**
     Connecting with Technology
       (Computer Spell Checks)

**21**    ph
     **STRATEGY:** Proofreading—Read Out Loud    **82**
     Focus on Language (Opposites—Antonyms)

**22**    ou
     **STRATEGY:** Make an Acrostic    **86**
     Focus on Language
       (Naming Words—Nouns)

| Lesson | | Page |
|---|---|---|
| **23** | **Hard and Soft g** <br> STRATEGY: Proofreading—Share It! <br> Focus on Language <br> (A Quick Guide—Dictionary Skills) | **90** |
| **24** | **SPELL CHECK (Review, Lessons 19–23)** | **94** |
| **25** | **ir, or, ur** <br> STRATEGY: Pronounce Words Clearly <br> Focus on Language (Alliteration) | **96** |
| **26** | **pr- and ex-** <br> STRATEGY: Build Word Families by Sound <br> Connecting with Science (Animal Collectives) | **100** |
| **27** | **Suffix -ed** <br> STRATEGY: Snap, Clap, Tap!—Syllables <br> Focus on Language <br> (Dictionary Sections) | **104** |
| **28** | **Suffixes -less and -able** <br> STRATEGY: Remember!—Mnemonic Devices <br> Focus on Language (Contractions) | **108** |
| **29** | **-y, -ay** <br> STRATEGY: Find a Word in a Word <br> Focus on Language (Irregular Plurals) | **112** |
| **30** | **SPELL CHECK (Review, Lessons 25–29)** | **116** |

## Extra-Challenge Lessons

| | | |
|---|---|---|
| **31** | **Silent Letter Review** <br> STRATEGY: Words Alive!—Use the Thesaurus <br> Connecting with Literature <br> (The Velveteen Rabbit) | **118** |
| **32** | **Homophone Review** <br> STRATEGY: Proofreading—Does It Look Right? <br> Connecting with Social Studies <br> (What's in a Name?) | **122** |

## Extra-Challenge Activities

| | |
|---|---|
| **Spelling Stretch** | **126** |
| **WORD LIST** | **143** |

# About Your Nelson Spelling Book

Here are the features in your spelling book that will help you become a better speller.

## Spelling Patterns

Each **Lesson** looks at a spelling pattern. A poem, short prose piece, or picture will show you some words that have the spelling pattern.

## Your Lesson Words

In each lesson you will use the **Word Box** to make a list of **Lesson Words** with the pattern you will be learning to spell. Sometimes we will include a few challenge words that we often find difficult to spell. You will be keeping your own **Personal Dictionary List** of words to use during your own reading, writing, and spelling.

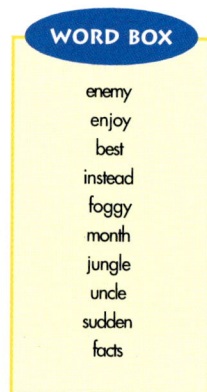

WORD BOX

enemy
enjoy
best
instead
foggy
month
jungle
uncle
sudden
facts

## Zoom in on Your Words

Activities, puzzles, and games will help you learn the meaning and spelling of words. You will practise your Lesson Words and learn new words.
**TRY THIS!** announces an extra challenge you may want to try.
You will be doing an activity **AT HOME**. Sometimes you will be asking someone at home to help you.

## Spelling Strategies

**STRATEGY SPOT** — Proofreading — Read Out Loud

The Strategy Spot in every lesson offers you ways to learn how to spell or proofread. Strategies are the tools that good spellers use. You can use these strategies when you are writing your own stories.

## Grammar

**Focus on Language** ▶ **Capital Letters**

**Focus on Language** gives you information and activities on English grammar. You can use these activities during writing time.

### Connecting with ... Other Subjects

Here you will find activities that help you use spelling strategies in reading, writing, and completing projects in other school subjects.

### A Focus on Your Own Reading and Writing

**Connecting with Literature** activities and the poems and short prose pieces included throughout your book will let you study words in authentic reading situations.

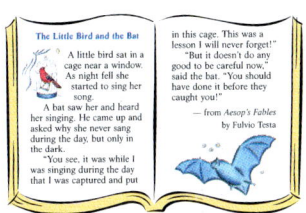

**SPELL CHECK** Every sixth lesson is a review of the spelling patterns and strategies you have been learning. You will be using the Lesson Words you still need to practise in games, puzzles, and other activities.

**Quick Tips** will give you useful information and tips about patterns and meanings of words. You can use these tips right away in the lesson!

**QUICK TIP**

**DID YOU KNOW?** will tell you interesting information about how our language grew and how it works.

**FLASHBACK**

How would you describe yourself as a speller? What are 2 things you would like to learn this year about spelling?

**Flashback** is a quiet time at the end of each lesson to think over what you have learned.

**Spelling Stretch** is a special section of exciting games and challenges in the back of this book. Find out more about words and make your spelling skills stretch.

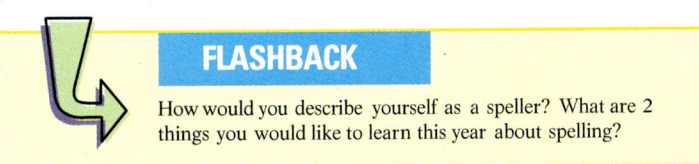

# 1 Short Vowel Sounds

Enjoy reading this poem about fast food for frogs!

**Fast Freddy**

Freddy froggy found fast food
For frogs was fun to eat.
Fast Freddy flicked his tongue for flies,
A fascinating feat.

And Freddy's flies were flavourful,
Both fresh and all for free.
How fortunate for Freddy frog —
A frugal frog was he.

— Ann McKay

## Creating Your Word List

**WORD BOX**

- enemy
- enjoy
- best
- instead
- foggy
- month
- jungle
- uncle
- sudden
- facts

**Say these words:**

fast   sent   will   top   bug

Listen to the **vowel sound** in each word. What is the same about all of the **vowel sounds**?

1. As a class, make a list of words that have the **short vowel sound**. Use the poem at the top of this page to help you. Put the words into a chart like this:

| a | e | i | o | u |
|---|---|---|---|---|
|   |   |   |   |   |

2. Work with your teacher to create the list of **short vowel** words you will be learning to spell.
You can use: the Word Box, the poem, your own words.
These are your Lesson Words.

3. **In your notebook**
   - Write the Lesson Words and mark each **short vowel sound** with the sign ˘. Do it like this:

     cĕntre, făcts
   - A Personal Dictionary will help in your reading and writing. You may want to add some of these **short vowel** words to your Personal Dictionary List.

**STRATEGY SPOT**

**Make a Rhyming Word**

When you are writing and are not sure how to spell a word, think of a word you KNOW that rhymes. For example: soggy – foggy, best – west. If you can spell the rhyming word, try spelling the first word.

# Zoom in on Your Words

1. **Missing Letters** Help! The computer is about to crash! It keeps missing letters. Fill in the missing letters to make words that have the **short vowel sound**. You will find most of these words in the Word Box.

   a) _ nj _ y    b) f _ g _ y    c) i _ st _ _ _
   d) _ _ cle     e) m _ _ th     f) j _ ng _ _

2. **Finding Vowels** Freddy's hungry again! Read the poem on page 8 again. How many **short vowel** words can you find now?

3. **Time to Rhyme Words** Rhyme each of these words:
   a) best   b) plug   c) snap   d) jungle   e) frill

## QUICK TIP

Which headline is stronger?
**Frightened Doggie Nips Letter Carrier.**
**Dog Bites Man.**
A short, bold headline grabs your attention and is easier to remember.

4. **Matching Word Pairs** Use words from the Word Box to complete these pairs in your notebook.
   a) **Woman** is to **man** as **aunt** is to ──────.
   b) **Day** is to **week** as ────── is to year.
   c) **Whale** is to **ocean** as **monkey** is to ──────.
   d) **Big** is to **biggest** as **good** is to ──────.
   e) **Love** is to **hate** as **friend** is to ──────.

5. **From Apples to Z ...** Work with a partner to make an alphabet for young children. Find a word with a **short vowel sound** for each letter of the alphabet. Make your list like this:

   a – **a**pple, b – **b**etter, c – **c**amel, d – **d**ig ...

   **TRY THIS!** For an extra challenge, try to have all of the words be on one theme. For example, try to find all food words or all animal words.

### DID YOU KNOW?
The English language is about 1500 years old, but Chinese is over 3000 years old.

**AT HOME**

6. **A Wordy Collage** Look through old magazines or newspapers to find **short vowel** words. Carefully cut out the words and arrange them on a piece of paper. Once you have an arrangement you like, glue the words onto the piece of paper to make a collage. Give your collage a title. Add any pictures you want that go with the words.

7. **What's in a Name?** Think of 5 names that have **short vowel sounds**. Write them down and mark each **short vowel sound**. Like this:

   Ăli

## FLASHBACK

How would you describe yourself as a speller? What are 2 things you would like to learn this year about spelling?

# Connecting with MATH

## Snack Surveys

**What kind of snacks do you like? Do you like licorice?**

1. Do a class licorice favourites survey. What kind of licorice — strings, nibs, or twizzlers — do people in your class like best? What are the favourite colours? Put all of this information on a graph.

2. What are your 3 favourite kinds of candy? Ask 3 friends what their favourites are. Put all of this information on a graph. Give the graph a title.

3. At home, you can ask your family and friends about their favourite kinds of candy. Draw a picture of the all-time favourite candy and write a tasty headline telling about it.

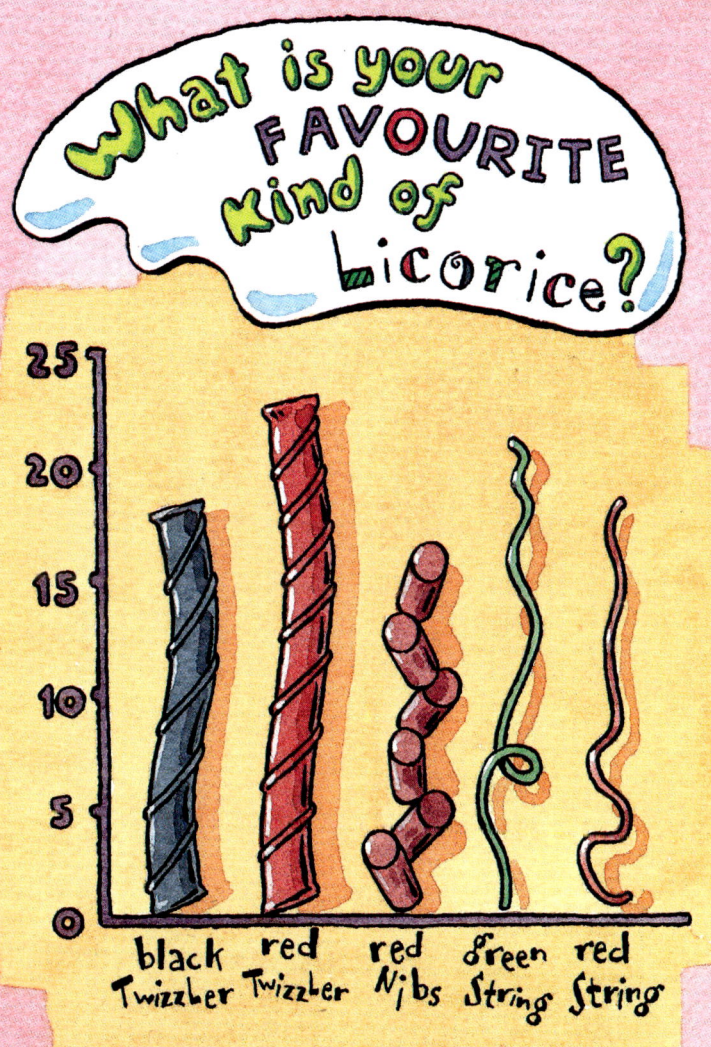

# 2 Long a

Remember this rainy-day rhyme?

Rain, rain, go away.
Come again another day.
Not in April, not in May,
Not a day I want to play.

## Creating Your Word List

**WORD BOX**

- able
- cage
- painter
- paid
- radio
- strange
- stairs
- playground
- stayed
- waited

**Say these words:**

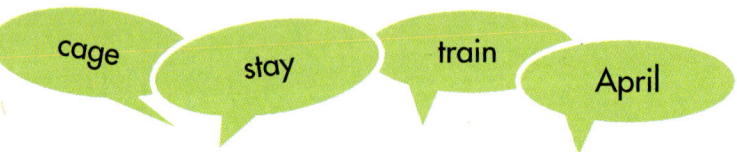

What sound do these 4 words have in common?

1. As a class, make a list of words that have the **long a sound**. Use the rhyme at the top of this page to help you.
   - Find the different ways to spell the **long a sound**. Write them down.
   - Put the words into a chart like this:

   | a + e | ai | ay | a | other |
   |-------|----|----|---|-------|
   |       |    |    |   |       |
   |       |    |    |   |       |

2. Work with your teacher to create the list of **long a** words you will be learning to spell.
   You can use: the Word Box, the poem, your own words.
   These are your Lesson Words.

3. **In your notebook**
   - Write the Lesson Words and mark the **long a sound** with the sign ¯.

- Keep adding new **long a** words to your Personal Dictionary List. Keep it up to date to help in your reading and writing.

## STRATEGY SPOT: Say It S...l...o...w...l...y

Saying a word slowly often helps you spell it. Say these words slowly and carefully: **painter, radio**.

1. Be a slowpoke! Read over your Lesson Words and say each word to yourself very slowly. Listen for each sound.

2. Sometimes it helps to ask a friend to say the word, because you may be skipping a sound.

# Zoom in on Your Words

**QUICK TIP**

Here are 3 unusual ways to spell the **long a sound**:
- **ea** like br**ea**k,
- **ei** like n**ei**ghbour,
- **ey** like th**ey**.

1. **Word Sort** Sort these words into 2 groups — **long a** and **short a**: tail, water, grade, jays, flat, break, have, neighbour, rabbit.
   ★ Put a star beside the words that gave you a problem.
   **TRY THIS!** For an extra challenge, use each problem word in an interesting sentence.

2. **Disappearing Letters** Print your Lesson Words and leave blanks for some of the letters. Like this:

   s t _ a _ g _

   Now have a partner go back and fill in the missing letters.

3. **Scrambled Words** Unscramble the following **long a** words. The Word Box will help you find most of the words.
   - a) ssarti
   - b) itreapn
   - c) aiodr
   - d) ifar
   - e) edwait
   - f) elba
   - g) gcae
   - h) gnertsa
   - i) yMa
   - j) idpa
   - k) ypgolarndu
   - l) adtesy

13

**4. Hidden Words** Draw a picture like the one below to illustrate your Lesson Words.

**5. Is There Rain in a Rainbow?** The word **air** is the **root word** for many longer words:

**air**plane, **air**y, **air**port, **air**way

The word **rain** is also the root for many words:

**rain**bow, **rain**y, **rain**fall, **rain**drop.

Say each word above and really STRESS the root word. Write each word and underline the root word.

**6. The Fare to the Fair** **Homophones** are words that sound the same but are spelled differently and have different meanings. Here are some examples of homophones:

I know the **way** to the park.  Do you **weigh** more than 32 kg?
That was a **fair** game.      The bus **fare** is 75 cents.

Write down the homophones above and draw a little picture beside each one. Start a class list of homophones.

**7. Long a Jeopardy** Pick a Lesson Word and write clues to describe it. For example: They help you get to the second floor. Answer: What are **stairs**? Read your clues to a partner and see if he or she can guess your Lesson Word. **TRY THIS!** For an extra challenge, do this with 3 Lesson Words.

8. **New-Word Machine** Switch on the new-word machine. Use each **root word** to make a new word. For example:

**brave – bravery**

a) paint – _____
b) day – _____
c) play – _____
d) mail – _____
e) base – _____
f) sail – _____
g) fair – _____
h) wave – _____
i) nation – _____

AT HOME

9. **Be a Word Detective!** Look around your house to find **long a** words. Look in the kitchen, the bedroom, the living room. List 15 **long a** words from your home. Which room had the most **long a** words?

# Focus on Language  Sentence Types

Different types of sentences make our stories interesting. There are:

- **statements:** It is raining.
- **questions:** Where is my raincoat?
- **exclamations:** Don't slip on the wet sidewalk!

1. Look at a picture in a book, a magazine, or the picture on page 14.

2. Make up a statement, a question, and an exclamation for the picture. Remember to use the correct punctuation! Label each sentence as a **statement**, **question**, or **exclamation**.

## FLASHBACK

What are some letters or patterns that make English tricky to spell? What is a good way to remind yourself to say all of the sounds in a word?

# 3  Long e

Have you ever been to the circus to see these performers?

**The Acrobat**

I'll swing
By my ankles,
She'll cling
To your knees
As you hang
By your nose
From a high-up
Trapeze.
Just one thing, please,
As we float through the breeze —
Don't sneeze.

— Shel Silverstein

## Creating Your Word List

**WORD BOX**

knee
sweep
deep
secret
key
pleased
easy
leaves
between
beak

**Say these words:**

knees   please   ceiling   key   trapeze

What sound do these 5 words share?

1. Make a list of words that have the **long e sound**. Use the poem to help you.
   - Look at the different ways the **long e sound** is spelled. Write them down.
   - Put the words into a chart like this:

| ee | ea | ey | e | e + e |
|----|----|----|---|-------|
|    |    |    |   |       |

2. Work with your teacher to create the list of **long e** words you will be learning to spell.
   You can use: the Word Box, the poem, your own words. These are your Lesson Words.

3. **In your notebook**
   Write the Lesson Words and circle any part of a word that gives you problems. Like this:

   e(a)s y      s e c(re)t

   Add new **long e** words that you find in your reading and writing to your Personal Dictionary List.

## STRATEGY SPOT

### Does It Look Right?

**When you are not sure how to spell a word, write it 2 different ways. Then circle the way that looks right. For example, which word looks right: sheep, or sheyp?**

Try this strategy with some of your Lesson Words. Write each word 2 different ways. Give the pairs of words to your partner.

Have him or her circle the word that looks right in each pair. Check the words to see if your partner chose correctly.

# Zoom in on Your Words

1. **Checkup!**  Have a partner dictate your Lesson Words to you.
   • Write down each word as your partner reads it out loud.
   • Check your words and correct any spelling mistakes.
   ★ Put a star beside the words that gave you a problem.
   **TRY THIS!** For an extra challenge, use each problem word in an interesting sentence.

2. **Wordprints**  A footprint shows the shape of a foot. A **wordprint** shows the shape of a word. Draw the shape of each of your Lesson Words. For example:

3. **Rhyme Time**  Find the **long e** words in this rhyme and add them to the chart from page 16.
   She sells seashells on the seashore.

4. **Fancy That!** Look at the words from the Word Box that gave you problems. Softly say each word to yourself. Print each word using fancy letters.

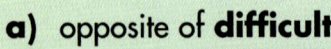

5. **Word Pole Acrobat** Copy and complete this Word Pole. Use the clues to write **long e** words. When you are done, the word in the pole will name something that flies.

a) opposite of **difficult**
b) it comes at the end of a sentence
c) what you do with books
d) done with a broom
e) they fall from trees in Autumn
f) what someone does to help you learn
g) they speak this in Japan
h) very odd

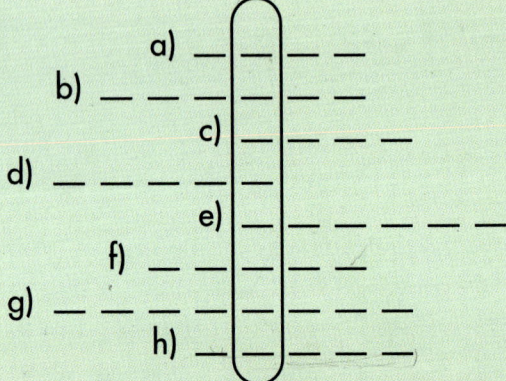

AT HOME

6. **TV Words** Find 10 **long e** words in your TV listings guide at home. Write them down and bring them to class tomorrow.

7. **A, B, C, and On and On ...** Put the words in each row in alphabetical order.
   a) easy, leaves, deep, pleased, knee
   b) sudden, enemy, foggy, month, jungle
   c) delay, radio, strange, cage, able

## FLASHBACK

Do you use your Personal Dictionary List during story writing?

# Connecting with Literature

### The Little Bird and the Bat

A little bird sat in a cage near a window. As night fell she started to sing her song.

A bat saw her and heard her singing. He came up and asked why she never sang during the day, but only in the dark.

"You see, it was while I was singing during the day that I was captured and put in this cage. This was a lesson I will never forget!"

"But it doesn't do any good to be careful now," said the bat. "You should have done it before they caught you!"

— from *Aesop's Fables* by Fulvio Testa

**1.** A **fable** is a story with a lesson. Draw a picture for this fable and write below it what you think the little bird learned.

**2.** Write down the titles of 10 songs you like. Put them in a list and add a title.

**3.** What does the expression **"As night fell"** mean? Write another way to say this. Have fun and draw a picture of the "night falling."

**4.** Put these words from the fable in alphabetical order.

sing, bird, replied, fable, dark, lesson

# 4 Long i

Read this high-flying poem.

**Catching the Clouds**

It's high time I fly my kite.
So bright and light in the sunlight,
Climbing, climbing, higher and higher.
Flying in the wild wind.

## Creating Your Word List

**WORD BOX**

- smiled
- died
- hike
- life
- might
- right
- child
- hiding
- kind
- mind

**Say these words:**

hike   idea   might   child   kind

What sound do these 5 words share?

1. Make a list of words that have the **long i sound**. The poem at the top of this page will help you.
   - What are the different ways to spell the **long i sound**? Write them down.
   - Put the words into a chart like this:

| i + e | igh | ind | ild |
|---|---|---|---|
|  |  |  |  |

2. Work with your teacher to create the list of **long i** words you will be learning to spell.
   You can use: the Word Box, the poem, your own words. These are your Lesson Words.

3. **In your notebook**
   - Write the Lesson Words and use the sign ⁻ to mark the **long i** vowel.
   - Keep this list nearby. You may want to add some of these **long i** words to your Personal Dictionary List.

## STRATEGY SPOT

### Look for Silent e

The letter **e** at the end of a word changes the vowel sound from **short** to **long**. For example: bit – bite, fin – fine, rid – ride.

# Zoom in on Your Words

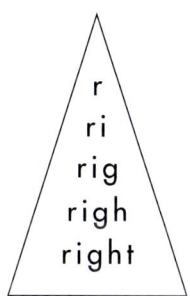

1. **Rhyming Words** Look at your Lesson Words. See if you can think of a word that rhymes with each Lesson Word.

2. **Word Pyramid** Choose a Lesson Word that you need to practise spelling. Draw a triangle in your notebook. On the first line, print the first letter of the word. On the second line, print the first 2 letters. On the third line, the first 3 letters. Continue until the triangle is full. Build a word pyramid with 2 other Lesson Words.

3. **Spelling Tic-Tac-Toe** Each person must use a different-coloured pencil. Player A prints a Lesson Word in 1 square on a tic-tac-toe board. Player B then prints a Lesson Word on the same tic-tac-toe board. Keep adding words until a player has 3 words in a row.

## QUICK TIP

The letter **y** can also have the **long i sound**. For example: **by, my, eye, fly, spy**.

4. **Different Ways of Sorting** Write each Lesson Word on separate small pieces of paper. Think of different ways to sort your words: Sort by meaning, sort by spelling pattern, sort by **vowel sound**, sort by number of letters. Tell how you sorted the words.

> **DID YOU KNOW?**
> English has adopted many words from other languages. For example: **spaghetti** is Italian, **tortilla** is Spanish, **challah** is Hebrew, **croissant** is _____ .

5. **That Word Reminds Me of ...** Say the word **bicycle**. What 2 other words come to mind? Copy this Word Web and complete it using your own words.

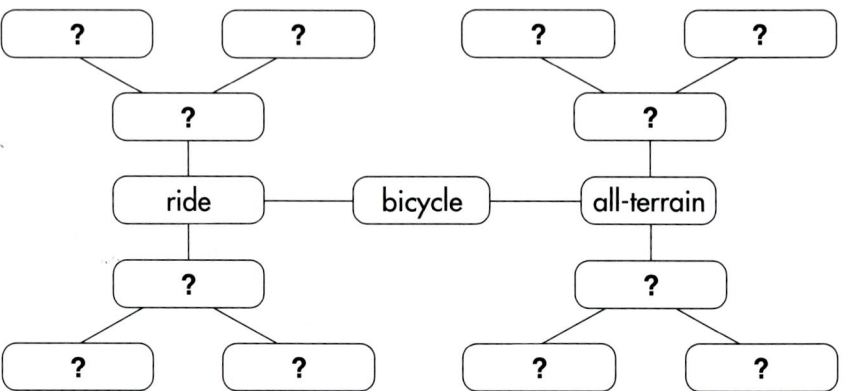

6. **What's in a Name?** Write down your name and 10 other names. Mark the long and short vowels in each name.

7. **Write the Right Knight Tonight — Homophones**
Some **long i** words are homophones: **write – right**, **hi – high**, **night – knight**. Write down each pair of homophones and draw a little picture beside each one.

# FLASHBACK

Look over all of the activities in this lesson. Which one helped you the most?

# Connecting with Literature

### The Frog and the Ox

A frog saw a big, strong ox near the pond.

"If only I were like that," he thought.

"Listen to him," commented a friend from among the reeds. "All he can do is dream about being bigger than he is."

The frog was so small that the ox did not see him. But the frog, who could see the ox very well, was so amazed by his size that he almost died of envy.

And so he puffed himself up as big as he could and asked the other frogs if he was now bigger than the ox.

"Not yet," they answered.

The frog puffed up again and asked once more, "Who — who is bigger now?"

"The ox," answered the frogs. Indignant, the frog tried again and puffed himself up still more. This time he puffed himself up so much that he actually split his skin.

"You see," remarked one of the other frogs, "there's no way you can make yourself any bigger than you actually are."

— from *Aesop's Fables* by Fulvio Testa

1. The words **envy**, **indignant**, **amazed**, **split**, and **puffed** help make the story interesting. What do these words mean?

2. Being someone else could be fun. But would it make life perfect? Try on someone else's life. Draw a picture of someone you would like to be and give 3 reasons why you would like to be the person. What are the advantages and problems of the person you would like to be?

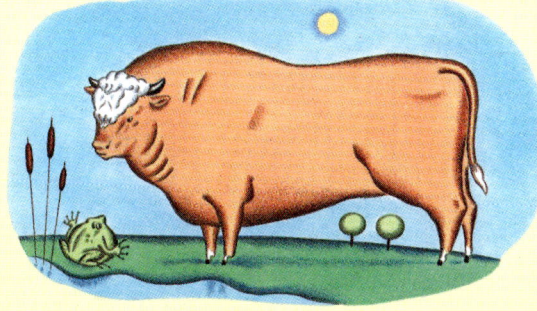

| Advantages | Problems |
|---|---|
|  |  |

# 5 Prefix un-

Unlock the locks by reading each word.

A **prefix** is a group of letters placed at the beginning of a word. The **prefix un-** can mean "not" or "opposite of."

**WORD BOX**

- unable
- unclean
- unpack
- uneven
- untie
- unfair
- unlock
- undo
- unlike
- unhappy
- untidy

## Creating Your Word List

1. Make a list of words that have the **prefix un-** at the beginning of the word. As you read each word in the list out loud, really STRESS the prefix **un-**.

2. Work with your teacher to create the list of **prefix un-** words you will be learning to spell.
   You can use: the Word Box, the diagrams, your own words. These are your Lesson Words.

3. **In your notebook**
   - Write the Lesson Words.
   - Highlight the parts you find difficult to spell.
   - Keep adding **un-** words to your Personal Dictionary List. Don't forget to keep it up to date.

## Zoom in on Your Words

1. **Not Roots** Write 5 of your **un-** Lesson Words. Beside each word, write the word **not** and the **root word**. Do it like this:

   unclean = **not clean**

2. **Wordprints** Draw the shape of each of your Lesson Words. For example:

   unlike  unhappy

3. **Alphabet Soup** Ready for some alphabet soup? With a partner, write down the letters of the alphabet on small pieces of paper. Do this 2 times. Make some extra vowels. Take turns picking letters. Who is the first one to make a word? Every time you make a word, you get 1 point. Who has the most points at the end of 10 minutes?

4. **Vowel Magician** Make vowels disappear! On the chalkboard or in your notebook, write a simple sentence and erase all of the vowels. Have a partner try to fill in the vowels so that the words make sense.

## STRATEGY SPOT
## Study Your Spelling Words

**There are many different ways to study your spelling words. Here are 6 ways.**

1. Many times a day, try to write the word from memory. Then check to see if you spelled it correctly.

2. Which part of the word is the hardest for you? Focus on this part. Say these letters with lots of force when you spell the word. For example: pro **bl** em.

3. Look at the word for 15 seconds. Close your eyes and see the word in your mind. Open your eyes, write the word, and then check to see if you were right.

4. Say the word in a way that will help you spell it. For example, say the word Val en **tine** with special emphasis on the difficult part.

5. Trace the letters of the word with your finger and say the letters as you trace.

6. Spell the letters in a musical way. Chant the letters and move your body as you sing.

Do you have your own special ways to study your words? Write them down and compare your strategies with a partner.

5. **Completing Sentences** Use an **un-** word to complete each of the following sentences in your notebook.

a) Keung told the doctor that he felt _____.
b) The pigs in the mud were very _____.
c) After the trip, Samira had to _____ her suitcase.
d) We were _____ to solve the computer problem.
e) The cause of some diseases is still _____.

| unpack |
| unwell |
| unclean |
| unknown |
| unable |

6. **Be a Word Cowpoke!** Write down each of your Lesson Words. "Lasso" the part of the word you need to practise spelling by drawing a circle around it. Close your eyes and silently spell each word to yourself. Check to see if you spelled it correctly.

7. **What's Another Word for Synonym?** Look at each of your Lesson Words. Think of another word that means the same. Words that mean the same are called **synonyms**. For example: **unwell = sick**. With your partner, find another word for each of your Lesson Words. Write down your words.

AT HOME

8. **Word Web** Pick 1 of your Lesson Words. What 2 words do you think of when you look at it? Now what 2 other words do you think of? Add as many words as you can to make a Word Web. For example:

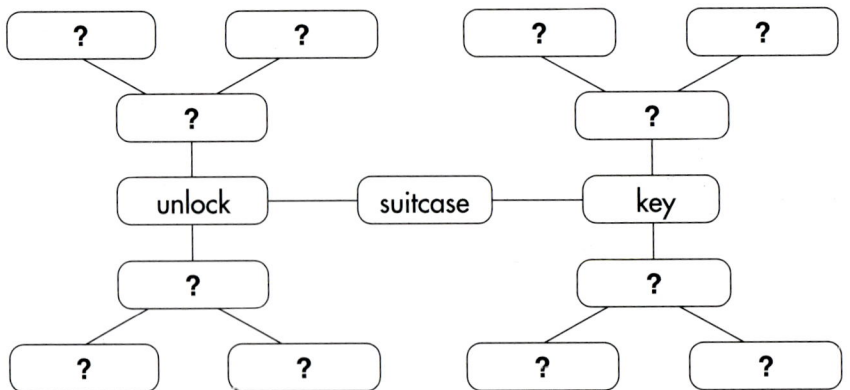

9. **Spotlight on Study Skills** Pick 5 Lesson Words that you find difficult to spell. Use the Strategy Spot on page 25 to help you learn these words. Tell one of your friends the ways that work best for you.

> **DID YOU KNOW?**
> How did Canada get its name? One story is that an Aboriginal chief, who was talking with the explorer Jacques Cartier, pointed to a village. Cartier thought the chief was pointing to the land all around. But the chief was really only saying his word for village. This word was "kanata."

# Focus on Language ▶ Action Words — Verbs

A **verb** is a word that shows action; for example: **honk**, **drink**, **shrink**, **throw**.

I can **throw** the ball.

1. Which of these words are verbs?

    drank, skunk, shrink, blink, honk, cranky

2. Go back to the Connecting with Literature story on page 23 in Lesson 4. Read the story and find 5 verbs.

3. Imagine you are in gym class. Make a list of 10 actions you can do in the gym.

    **TRY THIS!** For an extra challenge, use 3 of these verbs in sentences.

## FLASHBACK

Did you use a strategy when you were studying your Lesson Words? Which one? Did you work with someone else? You will find it helps sometimes to study with a partner.

# 6 SPELL CHECK

## REVIEW

**Patterns**

short vowel sounds
long a
long e
long i
prefix un-

**Strategies**

1. Make a rhyming word.
2. Say it slowly.
3. Does it look right?
4. Look for silent e.
5. Study your spelling words.

## Creating Your Word List

**In your notebook**
- Go to your list of "Words I Still Need to Practise."
- Pick 10 words you need to practise spelling.

## Zoom in on Your Words

1. **Say It Slowly**  S...l...o...w...l...y say each word to yourself and listen to every sound in the word.

2. **Underlining Letters**  Beside each word, write the letters you need to focus on. Like this:

    nation – <u>tion</u>, night – <u>gh</u>

    Use a coloured pencil to <u>underline</u> these tricky letters.

3. **v, c, or s?**  Is it the **vowels** or **consonants** you are not spelling correctly? Beside each word, write **v** for **vowel**, **c** for **consonant**, **s** for **silent letter** for each problem area.

4. **Mystery Letters**  Print your Lesson Words and leave blanks for some of the letters. Like this:

    eras _ r,  unk _ _ wn

5. **Vowel Check**  Use your Lesson Words to fill in this chart. (Some words may go in both columns.) Mark the vowels with the short and long signs.

| a) Short Vowel | b) Long Vowel |
| --- | --- |
|  |  |

**AT HOME**

6. **Practise Your Spelling Words**  Look at the Strategy Spot on page 25 of Lesson 5. Use the study skills to help you practise your Lesson Words.

7. **Word Search Puzzle**  Using a piece of graph paper, make a Word Search Puzzle with some of your Lesson Words. When you are finished, give it to someone else in the class to solve.

8. **Different Ways of Sorting**  Write each of your Lesson Words on a small piece of paper. Think of different ways to sort your words: Sort by meaning, sort by spelling pattern, sort by **vowel sound**. Sort your words different ways.

9. **Keep Your Place**  Make a bookmark to help you keep your place in this spelling book. Decorate it with fancy Lesson Words or any way you like.

10. **Climb Down the Letter Ladder**  Pick the longest Lesson Word you have. Write it in a column, from top to bottom. Use your other Lesson Words to fill in the ladder. Do it like this:

To fill in your ladder, you can use other words you know how to spell.

## FLASHBACK

Look at the Lesson Words you now know how to spell. Cross them off your list of "Words I Still Need to Practise." Give yourself a pat on the back for a job well done!

# 7 Long o

Have fun reading this fanciful poem out loud.

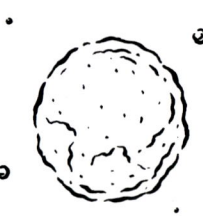

Tony swam across the Arctic Ocean,
Mariko rowed across all Seven Seas,
Nola rode a pony through the Gobi Desert,
But skating round Pluto — that's the trip for me!

## Creating Your Word List

**WORD BOX**

broken
coach
cone
hello
owner
post
rowing
smoke
sold
stones
whole

**Say these words:**

What **vowel sound** do these 5 words have in common?

1. As a class, make a list of words that have the **long o sound**. Use the poem at the top of this page to help you think of **long o** words.
   - Find the different ways to spell the **long o sound**. Write them down.
   - Put the words into a chart like this:

| o + e | oa | ow | – o | other |
|-------|----|----|----|-------|
|       |    |    |    |       |

2. Work with your teacher to create the list of **long o** words you will be learning to spell.
   You can use: the Word Box, the poem, your own words.
   These are your Lesson Words.

3. **In your notebook**
   - Write the Lesson Words and mark each **long o sound** with the **long vowel** sign ¯ over the letters.

   toast, whole

- You may want to add some of these **long o** words to your Personal Dictionary List. Your Personal Dictionary will help in your reading and writing.

# Zoom in on Your Words

1. **Wordprints** Fill in the letters in the following **wordprints** to make **long o** words

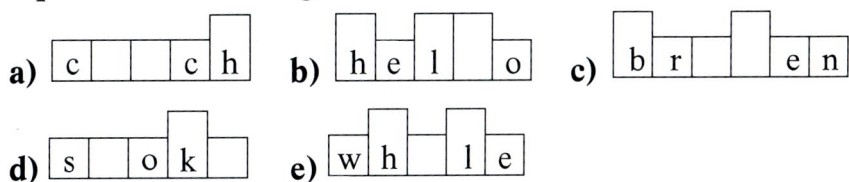

a) c _ c h   b) h e l _ o   c) b r _ _ e n
d) s _ o k   e) w h _ l e

**AT HOME**

2. **Word Sort** Write each of your Lesson Words on a small piece of paper. Think of different ways to sort your words: Sort by meaning, sort by spelling pattern, sort by **vowel sound**.

3. **From No to Go** Play Change-a-Letter. Change 1 letter in each of these words to make a new word.
   a) cone      b) post      c) bow
   d) boil      e) boat      f) hope

## STRATEGY SPOT — List Challenge Words

**English is a difficult language to learn to spell. Some words do not follow any spelling rules. For example, the words because and should are challenge words.**

1. Make a list of 3 words that are **challenge words**.
2. Look at your list of **challenge words**. Underline the parts of each word that you find EASY to spell. Say each word to yourself.
3. Add other **challenge words** to this list that you find.
4. Keep the list close by when you are writing stories so that you can check the spelling of these **challenge words**.
5. Show your list to someone at home and see what words cause her or him problems. Can you help that person spell 1 of these words?

31

**4. Be a "No" Poet!** With a partner, make a 1-word poem. One person says the word **No**. The second person responds by saying the word **No** in a different tone of voice. Keep going back and forth changing your voice. Now choose another **long o** word and try this poem again.

> **TRY THIS!** Do the poem with another **long o** word.

**5. Dinner for Four** **Homophones** are words that sound the same but are spelled differently and have different meanings. Some **long o** words are homophones:

> four – for, whole – hole, dough – doe, no – know

Write down each pair of homophones and draw a little picture beside each one. Add them to the class list of homophones. With a partner, can you think of 3 more **long o** homophones?

**6. Mixed-Up Sports Notes** The football coach has some notes for the players, but the words got mixed up. Help the coach by putting the words in order.

   a) zone. to Go end the
   b) the ball Hold score. can you until
   c) No the joking game. in
   d) and Joe. Stay follow low

> **TRY THIS!** For an extra challenge, make up a mixed-up note of your own for 1 of the football players for a partner.

**7.** **Bold, Bolder, Boldest!** Adding **-er** and **-est** to some words makes new words. Add **-er** and **-est** to some of these words. Be careful, not all of the words can have **-er** and **-est**!

  a) cold    b) bold    c) told
  d) sold    e) old     f) fold

**TRY THIS!** For an extra challenge, pick one **-er** and one **-est** word and use them in interesting sentences.

### DID YOU KNOW?

A **palindrome** is a word that can be spelled forwards or backwards. For example: **did**, **sees**, **peep**, **Dad**, **Mom**, **Bob**. Do you know any other palindromes?

# Focus on Language ▶ Descriptions

When you are writing sentences or stories, it sometimes helps to get a picture in your mind. Let's try it:

**1.** Get a picture in your head about any topic you like. Just daydream for a moment about that picture.

**2.** Now draw that picture. Add LOTS of detail. Make a list of **adjectives** that describe the picture.

**3.** Add lots of labels to describe the parts of the picture.

**4.** Use this picture and your list of adjectives in story-writing class to write a story.

## FLASHBACK

In this lesson, we looked at the **long o** spelling patterns and at **challenge words**. Has your list of challenge words helped you with your writing? Where do you keep your list of challenge words?

# 8 Long u

Dig into this juicy stew and find the **long u** words.

## Creating Your Word List

**WORD BOX**

- during
- June
- July
- pure
- huge
- fruit
- new
- flew
- use
- suit

**Say these words:**

What sound do these 4 words share?

1. Make a list of words that have the **long u sound**.
   - What are all the different ways to spell **long u**?
   - Put the words into a chart like this:

   | u + e | ew | ue | ui | other |
   |-------|----|----|----|-------|
   |       |    |    |    |       |

2. Work with your teacher to create the list of **long u** words you will be learning to spell.
   You can use: the Word Box, the illustration, your own words.
   These are your Lesson Words.

3. **In your notebook**
   - Write the Lesson Words and mark the **long u sound** with the sign ¯.
   - Keep adding new **long u** words to your Personal Dictionary List.

# Zoom in on Your Words

**QUICK TIP**

The word part **uni-** means "one." Words that begin with **uni-** have to do with the idea of "one." For example: **uni**form, **uni**cycle, **uni**corn, **uni**que, **uni**son.

1. **Hot Headlines** Create bold newspaper headlines using 3 of your Lesson Words. For example:

    HOT, HOT, HOT Heat wave in **July**

2. **Balloon Sort** Draw 5 blue balloons. Label each balloon with one of the **long u** spelling patterns. Use your balloons to sort these words:

    blue, use, few, true, suit, stew, huge, June, pure, grew, new, flew, glue, fruit, during

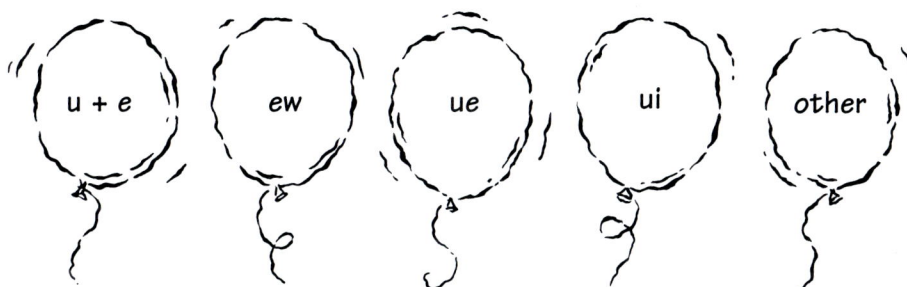

3. **Shape up!** Draw the **wordprint** shape of each of your Lesson Words. For example:

## STRATEGY SPOT — Draw Word Pictures

**Some words can be written in a way that helps us understand their meaning. For example:**

Choose 3 words and draw them in the shape of their meaning.

4. **ABC's of Long Vowels** Make an alphabet for young children. Write a word with a **long vowel sound** for each letter of the alphabet. Like this:

       **a** – **A**pril     **b** – **b**ike     **c** – **c**ute

> ### DID YOU KNOW?
> Some personal names come from different countries: **Jose** is a Spanish and Portuguese male name, **Keiko** is a female Japanese name, **Clara** is a female Italian name, and **Ajani** is a male Nigerian name.

AT HOME

5. **Finish Your Sentences** Copy down each of the sentence beginnings below. Complete the sentences at home. Read them to someone.
   a) July is a great month because …
   b) The huge gorilla …
   c) With a few dollars …
   d) Do not use …

6. **Ooh! What Can It Be?** Read this confusing poem.

       You can use it,
       You can lose it,
       You can buy it,
       You can fly it,
       You can glue it,
       You can fuse it,
       But don't ever try to chew it!

   What is this poem about? Draw a picture to tell what you think the poem is about. List all of the **long u** words in the poem.

## FLASHBACK

Complete each sentence: As a writer, I can … As a writer, I want to …

# Connecting with Art

## Word Collage

A **collage** is a picture made by gluing or taping many different photographs, objects, or pieces of fabric on a sheet of paper or Bristol board.

Let's make a word collage. Here's how you do it:

1. Look through magazines and newspapers to find interesting words. Look for different print styles.
2. Cut out the words. Sometimes cut closely around the letters, and at other times cut out the words in block form.
3. Once you have a collection of words, arrange them in different ways on a sheet of paper or Bristol board.
4. Once you have an interesting collage pattern, glue the words onto the page.
5. You may want to add a colourful title to your artwork. Show your collage to a partner.
6. Choose 4 of the words from your collage and use each one in a sentence.

You may want to add some of your collage words to your Personal Dictionary List.

# 9 kn-

Enjoy these goofy knock-knock jokes.

> Knock, knock.
> — Who's there?
> Ida.
> — Ida who?
> Ida know.
>
> Knock, knock.
> — Who's there?
> Eddy.
> — Eddy who?
> Eddy body home?

## Creating Your Word List

**Say these words:**

*knee* *knock* *know* *knife*

**WORD BOX**

- knock
- knife
- know
- knowing
- knit
- knapsack
- knob
- knot
- knuckle
- knight

What is the same in these 4 words?
All of the words have a **silent k**.

1. Make a list of words that have a **silent k** at the beginning of the word. Circle the **silent k** in each word.

2. Work with your teacher to create the list of **kn-** Lesson Words.
   You can use: the Word Box, the knock-knock jokes and your own words.
   Include these 2 **challenge words** in your Lesson Words:
   **friend, they**
   **Challenge words** are words that many people find difficult to spell.

3. **In your notebook**
   - Write the Lesson Words and circle each part of the word that gives you problems.
   - Keep your Personal Dictionary List up to date to help in your reading and writing.
   - Read the knock-knock jokes with a partner.
   
   **TRY THIS!** For an extra challenge, write your own knock-knock joke and share it with your partner.

## STRATEGY SPOT

### Highlight Beginning Sounds

It is a good idea to keep lists of words that begin the same way.

1. In your Personal Dictionary, list words that begin with the **kn-sound**. After you have written your words, say each one to yourself.

2. Find other groups of words that have the same beginning sound. Add them to your Personal Dictionary List.

# Zoom in on Your Words

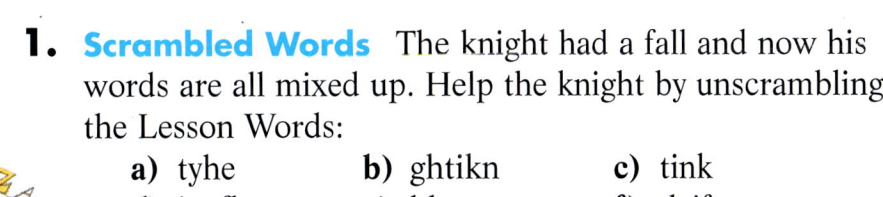

1. **Scrambled Words** The knight had a fall and now his words are all mixed up. Help the knight by unscrambling the Lesson Words:
   - a) tyhe
   - b) ghtikn
   - c) tink
   - d) ienfk
   - e) bkno
   - f) deifrn
   - g) nokt
   - h) okkcn
   - i) nkelkcu

2. **Silent Letters** Write down: **friend**, **knuckle**, **were**. Put an **X** through the silent letters in each word.

3. **Rhyme Time** Make rhyming words for 5 of your Lesson Words.

### DID YOU KNOW?

A long time ago, the silent **k** in words like **knight** and **know** used to be said aloud as part of the word. Say these words and pronounce the letter **k**. How does that sound?

**AT HOME**

4. **What Do You Know How to Do?** Write about a topic you know about. It could be a sport, a hobby, or a TV show. Make a poster or tell a story or make a list of facts.

5. **Exploding Roots!** Watch the word **know** "explode"!

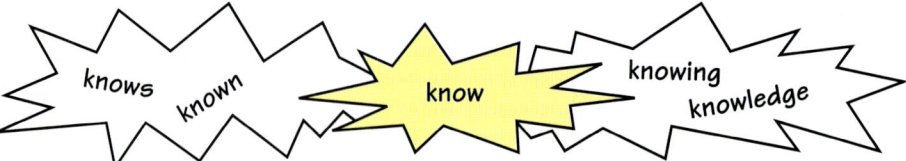

All of the new words have the same **root word** — **know**. Write them down and underline the root word **know**. Now complete each of these sentences.
   a) I know how to …
   b) My friend knows …
   c) It is well known that …
   d) Knowing how to …

6. **What's in My Knapsack?** **Knapsack** is another word for **backpack**. Do you have a knapsack? Write a story to describe where you would go with it. List all the things you would carry in it.

7. **Good Night, Knight** **Night** and **knight** are **homophones**. Write down the 2 homophones and draw a small picture beside each one. Add the words to your class list of homophones.

8. **Alphabet Soup** With a partner, write down the letters of the alphabet on small pieces of paper. Do this 2 times. Make some extra vowels. Take turns picking letters. Who is the first one to make a word? Every time you make a word you get a point. Who has the most points at the end of 10 minutes?

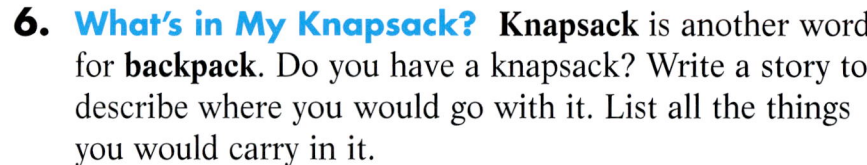

## FLASHBACK

When you have an At Home spelling activity, where do you do it? (At the kitchen table? In front of the television?) When do you do it? Who can you ask for help? What is a good time to do it?

# Connecting with
# PHYSICAL EDUCATION

## Sports Mobile

She shoots, she scores!
It's going, going, gone!
Slam, dunk!
Touchdown!

Let's make a sports mobile.
Follow these steps:

1. As a class, make a list of sports.

2. Do a survey to find out the class favourites.

3. Every sport has different equipment, rules, cheers, and superstars. Choose a sport that you play or would like to play. Find out all you can about that sport. Use some of your spelling strategies to spell words you find that are difficult.

4. Put the information and pictures onto small pieces of construction paper (10 cm x 10 cm).

5. You may have to check the spelling of some of these words. Have a friend read over your cards to check your spelling.

6. Put a title on each sheet. Include pictures and words. Then string the papers and pictures onto a hanger to make a mobile.

# 10 sh

How fast can you say these 2 tongue twisters without slipping up?

Sheep shouldn't sleep in a shed.

"Go, my son, and shut the shutter."
"I cannot shut it any shutter."

## Creating Your Word List

**WORD BOX**

shady
shell
shine
shiny
should
shark
shower
splash
wishful
wishes

**Say these words:**

What is the same in these 4 words?
All of the words begin with **sh**.

1. Make a list of words that have the **sh sound**. Use the tongue twisters to help you. As you read each word in the list out loud, really STRESS the **sh sound**.

2. Work with your teacher to create the list of **sh** words you will be learning to spell.
   You can use: the Word Box, the tongue twisters, your own words.
   These are your Lesson Words.

3. **In your notebook**
   • Write the Lesson Words and underline the **sh sound**.
   • You may want to add some of these **sh** words to your Personal Dictionary List.
   • Take turns with a partner reading each of the tongue twisters out loud 3 times. See who can read them the fastest.
   
   **TRY THIS!** Write your own **sh** tongue twisters.

## STRATEGY SPOT

### Make a Foldover

**Here is a fun way to practise spelling Lesson Words. It's called a foldover.**

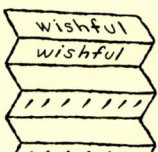

1. Pick a Lesson Word you want to practise.
2. Fold a piece of paper like a fan. Make six folds.
3. Print a Lesson Word on the first fold.
4. Fold over so you can't see the word.
5. On the next fold write the word again.
6. Open up the paper and check your spelling.
7. Use the foldover strategy with 2 other Lesson Words. Be sure to check the correct spelling of each word.

## QUICK TIP

**Sh** is called a **digraph**. It can be at the beginning, middle, or end of a word. For example: **sh**ip, bi**sh**op, ru**sh**.

# Zoom in on Your Words

1. **Words in Words**  Can you hear the **sea** in seashells? Write your Lesson Words. Find smaller words in the Lesson Words. Circle the smaller words.

2. **Missing Letters**  That shaky old computer needs a tune-up. It keeps missing some of the letters. Print 6 of your Lesson Words and leave blanks for some of the letters. Like this:

    s _ eep,   she _ l ,   _ how _ r

    Now go back and fill in the missing letters.

3. **Word Spiral**  Draw a spiral in your notebook. In the middle, print the first letter of a Lesson Word you want to practise. Print the word over and over, around the spiral. Do this with a second Lesson Word you want to practise.

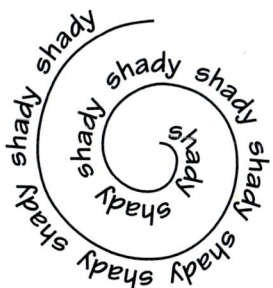

43

4. **Gone Fishing!** Copy the word pole and use the clues to write Lesson Words. The word in the pole will show you something to celebrate.

a) a kind of fish
b) you do this with soap and water
c) found on the beach
d) a flashlight does this
e) rhymes with **could**
f) under a tree it is …
g) polish it until it is …

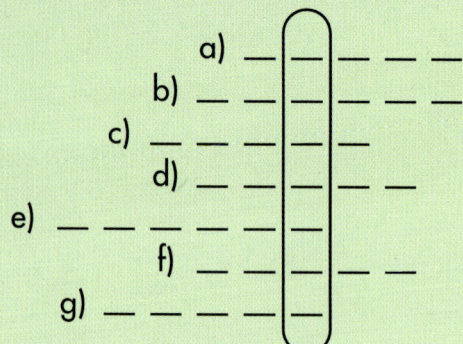

AT HOME

5. **In the Shade of a Shady Tree**

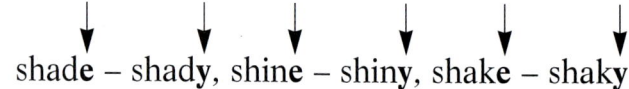

shad**e** – shady, shin**e** – shiny, shak**e** – shaky

Notice how the **e** changes to **y**.

Use **shade**, **shady**, **shine**, or **shiny** to fill in the blanks.
 a) On a hot day I look for a _____ spot.
 b) The glass was so _____ I could see myself in it.
 c) The big, old tree gives lots of _____ .
 d) First I wash and wax the car, then I _____ it.

6. **Shush! We're Playing Concentration**

Cut a sheet of paper into 20 equal-sized squares. Write your Lesson Words twice — 1 word per square. Turn the squares over, and then mix them up. Number the **back** of the squares from 1 to 20. Lay the squares down so that the numbers are showing. Take turns turning over any 2 numbers until you get a pair of matching words.

# Focus on Language ▶ Word Shortcuts — Contractions

A **contraction** is a word shortcut. It is 2 words shortened to 1 word. An **apostrophe** (') shows that 1 or more letters have been left out of a word. Read these contractions and their long forms:

| | |
|---|---|
| cannot | **can't** |
| I have | **I've** |
| she is | **she's** |
| they are | **they're** |
| we will | **we'll** |
| he will not | **he won't** |

Write a **contraction** to replace the **bold** words in each sentence.

1. This year **I am** studying dinosaurs in science.

2. **I have** talked to an expert at the museum. **She is** a scientist who studies dinosaurs.

3. She **cannot say** for sure why the dinosaurs died out. They probably **were not** able to adapt to a sudden change in the weather.

4. Dinosaurs **could not** find the plants that they had been eating.

5. **We are** sure of one thing — **they are** no longer living on earth.

6. I **do not** think people will become extinct like the dinosaurs. **We will** protect our environment.

## FLASHBACK

When you are writing a story, which spelling strategies do you use? Look through this speller and find another 1 or 2 strategies you can try when story writing.

# 11 qu

Have fun reading this poem out loud. Read it quickly!

**The Question Queen**

Quick, quick,
the Queen is coming.
Quiet now —
she'll soon be here!

Stop your quarrels,
prepare your questions.
She's very clever,
that is quite clear.

Quiz her gently,
quiz her hard.
The Question queen —
she'll answer all!

# Creating Your Word List

**WORD BOX**

quick
quickly
quiet
question
Quebec
quilt
quarter
quail
square
squeeze

**Say these words:**

quack    quiz    quote

What sound is made by **qu** in each word?

1. Make a list of words that have the **qu sound**. Use the poem "The Question Queen" to help you. As you read the poem out loud, STRESS the sound made by each of the **qu** words.

2. Work with your teacher to create the list of **qu** words you will be learning to spell.
   You can use: the Word Box, the poem, your own words.
   Circle the **qu sound** in each Lesson Word.

**3. In your notebook**
- Write the Lesson Words.
- Highlight the parts of the words you find difficult.
- Keep adding **qu** words and **challenge words** to your Personal Dictionary List.

## STRATEGY SPOT

### Proofreading

To **proofread** means to check what you have written. Proofreading is important because it helps you find your errors and produce the best work possible. Always proofread your work to check for spelling.

# Zoom in on Your Words

1. **Proofreading** Copy the Lesson Words, correcting the errors as you write down the words.

   a) qween   b) qick   c) kwilt
   d) qestion   e) quebec   f) qhail

2. **Test Yourself** Have a partner dictate your Lesson Words to you.
   - Write down each word as your partner reads it out loud.
   - Check your words and correct any spelling mistakes.
   ★ Put a star beside the words that gave you a problem.

3. **Missing qu** Fill in the missing letters to make **qu** words.

   a) q _ ite   b) qu _ _ n   c) _ u _ lt
   d) _ _ iz   e) _ _ iet   f) s _ _ eeze

   Read the new words out loud to yourself.

4. **Match-Up Quiz** Match the words with their meaning clues.

   1) square       a) $\frac{1}{4}$
   2) quarter      b) a province
   3) Quebec       c) a small bird
   4) queen        d) a warm covering
   5) quick        e) royalty
   6) quilt        f) fast
   7) quail        g) a four-sided figure

**5. Run Quickly — Exploding Words!** Watch the word **squeeze** "explode"!

Explode the root words below by adding **-s**, **-ed**, **-ing**, **un-**. Write as many new words as you can. Use a dictionary to make sure each new word makes sense.

    **a)** quilt      **b)** quiet      **c)** square      **d)** question

**TRY THIS!** Use 3 of the new words in sentences.

**6. qu Sentences** Complete the following sentences using **qu** words.
    **a)** The _____ wore a brilliant crown.
    **b)** Please be _____ during the test.
    **c)** The duck _____ as it walked along the shore.
    **d)** _____ the tube to get the toothpaste out.
    **e)** The feather _____ keeps me warm in the winter.

**7. I'm Thinking of ...** Play "I'm Thinking of a Lesson Word" with a partner. Pick a Lesson Word. Give your partner a clue about the word. See if your partner can guess the word in 3 tries.

**DID YOU KNOW?**
The name for two babies is **twins**, for three babies, **triplets**, for four babies, **quadruplets**, and for five babies, **quintuplets**!

**8. A Homophone Is Not a Phone at Home!** The words **check** and **cheque** are homophones. **Check** means to "go over" and a **cheque** is a "money order." Use **check** or **cheque** to complete each sentence.
    **a)** Mother wrote a _____ to pay the bills.
    **b)** The teacher will _____ and return our notebooks.
    **c)** Put a _____ beside the finished items on the list.

# Focus on Language ▶ Capital Letters

**Capital letters** are used to start sentences:

> **T**he cheetah is the fastest land animal.

They also begin the name of a person, place, or particular thing:

> **R**oberta **B**ondar
> **C**orner **B**rook, **N**ewfoundland
> **T**he **N**ational **G**allery

1. Write the first and last names of 3 of your classmates.

2. Write the names of 2 places you would like to visit.

3. Correct these sentences by adding capital letters. **Proofread** your finished work.
   a) maria and david will come with me to the canadian museum of civilization.
   b) lisa will visit bermuda in may.
   c) edmonton is the capital city of alberta.

4. **Practise Your Spelling Words** Find and list 12 words with capital letters for people, places, or particular things in your neighbourhood.

## FLASHBACK

When you are proofreading your work, be sure to look for words that need capital letters.

# 12 SPELL CHECK

## REVIEW

**Patterns**

long o
long u
kn-
sh
qu

**Strategies**

1. List **challenge words**.
2. Draw word pictures.
3. Highlight beginning sounds.
4. Make a foldover.
5. Why proofread?

## Creating Your Word List

**In your notebook**
- Go to your list of "Words I Still Need to Practise."
- Pick 10 words you need to practise spelling.
- Beside each word, write the letters you need to focus on, like this:

coach – **oa**,  flew – **ew**

- Use a coloured pencil to underline these letters.

## Zoom in on Your Words

1. **Be a Slowpoke!** S…l…o…w…l…y say each word to yourself and listen to every sound in the word.

2. **Word Spiral** Draw a spiral in your notebook. In the middle, print the first letter of a Lesson Word you find difficult to spell. Print the word over and over along the spiral. Do this with a second word you find difficult to spell.

3. **Climb Down the Letter Ladder** Pick the longest Lesson Word you have. Write it in a column, from top to bottom. Use your other Lesson Words to fill in the ladder.

4. **What's in a Song Title?** Print the title of your favourite song on a piece of paper. Leave a space between the letters. Cut out the letters. Use these letters to write new words. You do not need to use all of the letters. You can use each letter as many times as you want.

AT HOME

5. **Practise Your Spelling Words** Look at the Strategy Spot on page 25 in Lesson 5. Use some of the ideas to help you practise your Lesson Words.

6. **Word Chain** See how long a word chain you can make. Write down a Lesson Word. Use the last letter of that word to start the next word. Like this:

Use other words you know to continue the chain.

7. **I'm Thinking of ...** Play "I'm Thinking of a Lesson Word" with a partner. Pick a Lesson Word. Give your partner a clue about the word. (Be careful not to say the Lesson Word!) See if your partner can guess the word in 3 tries.

8. **An Assortment of Sorts** Write each of your Lesson Words on small pieces of paper. Think of different ways to sort your words: Sort by meaning, sort by spelling pattern, sort by **vowel sound**.

9. **Foldover** Pick 3 Lesson Words you want to study and use the **foldover** strategy. See the Strategy Spot on page 43 of Lesson 10 for full directions.

10. **Concentration** Cut a sheet of paper into 20 equal-sized squares. Write your Lesson Words twice — 1 word per square. Turn the squares over, and then mix them up. Number the **back** of the squares from 1 to 20. Lay the squares down so that the numbers are showing. Take turns turning over any 2 numbers until you get matching words.

## FLASHBACK

Look at the Lesson Words you now know how to spell. Cross them off your list of "Words I Still Need to Practise." Take a bow — you are doing a great job!

# 13 nk

Do you notice signs and billboards like these when you are out for a drive?

## Creating Your Word List

**WORD BOX**

- drank
- skunk
- blank
- blink
- chunk
- drink
- shrank
- shrink
- trinket
- cranky

**Say these words:**

What sound is the same in these 3 words? Can you hear the **nk sound** in these words?

1. As a class, make a list of words that have the **nk sound**. Use the signs at the top of this page to help you. Really STRESS the **nk sound** as you read the words.

2. Work with your teacher to create the list of **nk** words you will be learning to spell.
   You can use: the Word Box, the signs, your own words.
   Include these 3 words:

   first, favourite, finally

   These 3 words are **challenge words**.

3. **In your notebook**
   - Write the Lesson Words.
   - Highlight the parts of the words you find difficult to spell.

- Keep adding **nk** words and **challenge words** to your Personal Dictionary List. Don't forget to keep it up to date to help in your reading and writing.

## STRATEGY SPOT: Highlight Letters That Need Attention

Often we can spell most of a word. Sometimes it is only 1 or 2 letters that need extra attention. Here are some ways to highlight these letters that need extra attention:

1. You can say the word out loud with extra EMPHASIS on the problem part.
2. You can <u>underline</u> the part that needs practice.
3. You can make up a rhyme. For example: "Don't **drink** the **ink**" reminds us that the easy word **ink** is inside the word **drink**.

Pick 3 Lesson Words that are difficult for you and try out these spelling strategies.

# Zoom in on Your Words

1. **Be a Word Cowpoke!** Write Lesson Words. "Lasso" any silent letters you find by drawing a circle around them.

2. **Missing Letters** Oops! The computer printer is on the blink again. It left blanks. Fill in the missing letters to make words. The Word Box will help you.

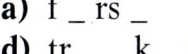

a) f _ rs _
b) fav _ _ r _ _ e
c) _ in _ l _ y
d) tr _ _ k _ t
e) _ ra _ ky
f) b _ i _ k
g) _ _ ra _ k
h) d _ an _
i) ch _ _ k

3. **Challenge Words** The words **first**, **favourite**, and **finally** are **challenge words**. S...l...o...w...l...y say each word to yourself and listen to every sound in the word. Close your eyes and spell the word softly to yourself. Open your eyes and check your spelling.

4. **"Baby Needs a Blanky"** Use **nk** words to fill in the blanks in these sentences.
   a) The _____ baby would not stop crying.
   b) The dust made my eyes _____ .
   c) Hot water makes wool _____ .
   d) The artist filled the _____ paper with colours.

AT HOME

5. **Favourite Things** Make a chart in your notebook.

**My Favourites**

| Books | TV shows | Music Groups |
|---|---|---|
| _____ | _____ | _____ |
| _____ | _____ | _____ |
| _____ | _____ | _____ |
| _____ | _____ | _____ |

Choose 3 categories, such as Books, TV Shows, and Music Groups. Make a list under each heading of your favourites for each category.

6. **First to Finally** Take a Word Trip. Copy the boxes in your notebook and follow the arrows to fill in the spaces. Choose a Lesson Word to start off the first box. Write a word you think of when you say the word in the box you just left. Print the word **first** in small letters above the first box, and **finally** above the last box.

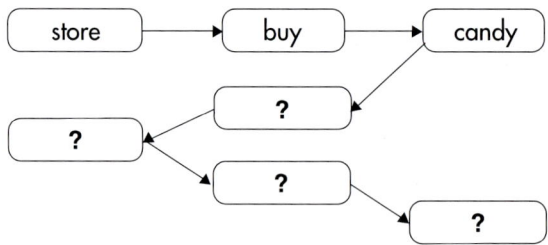

7. **Bumblebee** Play the Bumblebee game with a partner. Player A chooses a Lesson Word and writes down a dash for each letter of the word. Player B has to figure out the word by guessing 1 letter at a time. Only 1 guess of the final word is allowed. For every incorrect guess, Player A draws another part of the Bumblebee. Then switch roles. Watch out for that stinger!

**8. How Unusual!** The words **cranky** and **trinket** are not common words. As a class, find out what they mean. Use each word in a sentence.

> **DID YOU KNOW?**
> An **idiom** is an expression whose meaning cannot be understood simply from the words used. For example:
> a) it's raining cats and dogs   b) in hot water
> c) time flies   d) cut it out
> Read each idiom and try to figure out what it means.

# Focus on Language ▸ Getting Ideas

Authors can get ideas for writing from everyday events, people, books, TV programs, or the newspaper. They jot down ideas or make quick drawings and return to them later.

**1.** Keep a small Author's Notebook with you for a week. Write in it daily — a few words or sentences, maybe a drawing or two. You might even paste in a ticket stub, part of a magazine article, and so on.

**2.** Think of a book you like. What happened in the book?

**3.** List events that have happened to you.

**4.** See how many interesting **verbs** (action words) you can write down.

**5.** Use 1 or 2 of these ideas to develop a story.

**6.** The next time you need an idea for writing, just flip through your Author's Notebook.

## FLASHBACK

When you have a partner activity in spelling, do you always work with the same person? Next time work with someone else. When working with a partner, what are some things to remember to do so the activity goes smoothly?

# 14 ck

How fast can you say this tongue twister?

How much wood would a woodchuck chuck
If a woodchuck could chuck wood?
He would chuck
What wood a woodchuck could chuck
If a woodchuck could chuck wood.

## Creating Your Word List

**Say these words:**

**WORD BOX**

- attack
- brick
- dock
- track
- hockey
- lucky
- pocket
- thick
- ticket
- locket

What sound do these 3 words have in common? How would you describe the **ck sound**? Is it a "soft" sound? Is it a "hard" sound? Can you hear both the **c** and the **k**?

**1.** Make a list of words that have the **ck sound**. Use the tongue twister to help you. As you read each word in the list out loud, STRESS the **ck sound**.

**2.** Work with your teacher to create the list of **ck** words you will be learning to spell.
You can use: the Word Box, the tongue twister, your own words. These are your Lesson Words.

**3. In your notebook**
- Write the Lesson Words and underline the **ck sound**.
- You may want to add some of these **ck** words to your Personal Dictionary List.
- Take turns with a partner reading the tongue twister out loud 3 times. See who can read it the fastest.
- Look in an encyclopedia to find out what a woodchuck looks like and draw a picture of it. The woodchuck is also called a **groundhog**.

## STRATEGY SPOT

### Give It a Go! — Leave a Blank

**When you are writing and are not sure how to spell a word, spell as much of it as you can. For example, if you are not sure how to spell ticket, you might spell it like this: tic __ t. You can come back to the word later. Ask a friend to help you fill in the missing letters or check the dictionary, your Lesson Words, or Personal Dictionary List.**

# Zoom in on Your Words

1. **Give It a Go!** Work with a partner to practise the Give It a Go! spelling strategy. Have your partner dictate your Lesson Words to you. If you are not sure how to spell the whole word, draw a line for the missing letters. Correct your words.

2. **Extra! Extra!** Write down 3 Lesson Words that you find difficult. Underline the parts of the word that need extra attention.

3. **Going Blank** Print 7 of your Lesson Words and leave lines for some of the letters. Like this:

    ho _ ke _

    Now go back and fill in the missing letters.

4. **What Sorts?** With a partner, write all of your Lesson Words on little pieces of paper. Read over your words and think of different ways to sort them: Sort by meaning, by sound, by **silent letter**, and so on. You will not be able to use all your words for every sorting.

5. **Word Web** Pick 1 of your Lesson Words. What 2 other words come to mind? Add as many words as you can to make a Word Web. See an example of a Word Web on page 22 in Lesson 4.

## QUICK TIP

The **ck digraph** can be found in the middle or end of a word. No word in English begins with **ck**.

**6. Crossword Attack** Use the clues to attack this **ck** crossword. Write your answers in your notebook.

**Across**
2 opposite of **thin**
4 where boats arrive
5 it is often a heart shape
7 a game played with a stick and a puck
8 a guard dog will do this

**Down**
1 use this to build a house
3 a good place to put your money and keys
5 you have to be this to win the jackpot
6 you need this to get into the movies

**7. A Lock in the Locket!** Find small words inside these words:

a) attack   b) tackle   c) track   d) unpack
e) hockey   f) lucky    g) ticket  h) locket

AT HOME

**8. In My Pocket**

I wrote a letter to my friend,
And on the way I dropped it,
An old man picked it up again,
And put it in his pocket.
P-O-C-K-E-T
Pocket.

In your notebook, draw a pocket and write 10 things that can be found in someone's pocket. (Ask someone at home what is in his or her pocket.) Use the Give It a Go! spelling strategy on page 57 to help you with any words that are difficult.

### DID YOU KNOW?

As our world changes, we keep adding new words. For example, the computer words **interface, user-friendly, modem, E-mail,** and **Internet** have all been added to our language since 1950.

# Focus on Language ▶ Units of Sound — Syllables

A **syllable** is a "unit of sound." Words are made up of syllables — sometimes 1, sometimes more. Each syllable has at least **1 vowel** in it. In the example below the vowels are blue.

l**o**ck has 1 syllable
l**o**ck • **e**t has 2 syllables

**1.** Clap out the syllables for each of these words:

attack, block, trinket, unpack, struck, cranky, elephant, hockey, pocket, alligator

**2.** How many syllables are in your first and last name? How many syllables are in your teacher's name? How many syllables are in the name of your school?

**3.** Write words that have 1, 2, and 3 syllables.
TRY THIS! For an extra challenge, find words that have 4 and 5 syllables.
Here's a superchallenge! How many syllables are in this made-up word?

**supercallifragelisticexpyalidotious.**

## FLASHBACK

When you need help spelling a word, what do you do?
What are 3 things you can do to help yourself?

# 15 -tion

"Lights, camera, action!"

People making movies don't really say this. It's more like: "Scene 12, take 22. Rolling." **Rolling** means they're shooting film.

Have you ever wondered what these words meant at the end of a movie?

*gaffer:* Electrician in charge of the lights on a movie set.
*dolly:* A platform with wheels that carries a camera to different positions on the set.
*location:* A place where a film is shot away from a studio.
*post production:* What happens after the filming. This includes editing, completion of special effects, creation of titles, and addition of soundtrack music.

## Creating Your Word List

**WORD BOX**

- action
- addition
- collection
- direction
- information
- invention
- position
- education
- vacation
- pollution

**Say these words:**

addition   action   collection

What sound does **-tion** make?
If you were going to spell **-tion** the way it sounds, how would you spell it?

1. Make a list of words that have the **-tion sound**. Use the movie words and their definitions to help you.

2. Work with your teacher to create the list of **-tion** words you will be learning to spell.
   You can use: the Word Box, the movie words, your own words. These are your Lesson Words.

3. **In your notebook**
   - Write the Lesson Words and underline the **-tion** endings.
   - Keep adding new **-tion** words to your Personal Dictionary List.
   - A list of words and their definitions is called a **glossary**.

## STRATEGY SPOT

### See It — Visualize Words

When you visualize a word, you "see" in your mind what the word looks like.

1. Write down a Lesson Word.
2. Cover it with a sheet of paper.
3. Imagine you can still see the word. Try to get a picture of the word in your mind.
4. Uncover the word. Did you visualize the word?

Try this spelling strategy with 5 of your Lesson Words.

# Zoom in on Your Words

1. **Missing Letters** Fill in the missing letters to make **-tion** words. The Word Box will help you.
   a) ac _ i _ n     b) co _ _ ect _ o n     c) va _ at _ o _
   d) dir _ _ ti _ n     e) _ duc _ t _ _ n

2. **Syllable Count** The word **trans • por • ta • tion** has 4 **syllables**. Count the number of syllables in each of your Lesson Words.

## QUICK TIP

Nine out of 10 words that end with the sound **"shun"** are spelled with **-tion**.

3. **Invent an Invention** Change these verbs to nouns that end in **-tion**. For some words, you will need to add or change letters. If you need help, use a dictionary.
   - a) add
   - b) invent
   - c) direct
   - d) collect
   - e) inform
   - f) explore
   - g) pollute
   - h) celebrate

AT HOME

4. **Favourite Movie Action** Retell the story of your favourite movie.

> **DID YOU KNOW?**
> In 1455, **Johannes Gutenberg** invented a new way of printing using movable type. Before this, most books were written by hand. Once printing took over, **standard spelling** became common.

QUICK TIP

Words that end in –**tion** are **nouns**.

5. **Alphaspell** Play Alphaspell with a partner. Write down any 3 letters of the alphabet. Have your partner think up words for the letters. Like this:

   **SWG** — *Scores Winning Goal*

   Take turns giving each other alphabet letters.
   **TRY THIS!** For an extra challenge, use **-tion** words.

6. **Vacation in Mind** Close your eyes and visualize a vacation place. What do you see, hear, and smell? What can you do? Make a list of 10 words to tell about this vacation.

7. **Noun Hunt** Find the **nouns** in these sentences:
   - a) The scientist has a new invention.
   - b) My collection of cards is fantastic.
   - c) We must all try to stop pollution.
   - d) My vacation in Nova Scotia was great!

### FLASHBACK

How can you remember to spell the **-tion sound** correctly, and not write **"shun"**?

# Connecting with SCIENCE

What are you studying in science class? Look at the words and pictures in your science books. Think about what you have learned.

## Let's make a SCIENCE POSTER

Begin to design your poster on a piece of scrap paper:

1. Start by writing down 3 facts about your topic.
2. List 5 words that are special to the topic. Put them in a box on your poster.
3. Draw a picture about your topic, and give it a label.
4. Write 3 sentences about your topic. Add a title to your poster. Remember what you learned about writing short, bold titles and headlines.
5. Use your spelling strategies to learn words that are difficult.
6. Now you are ready to work on a good copy.
7. Don't forget to *proofread* the final copy of your poster.

Now you are ready to display your poster.

Have fun!

# 16 ch

Chant this poem:

> Charley went over the ocean,
> Charley went over the sea,
> Charley caught a codfish,
> But he can't catch me.

Try to make up your own chant using **ch** words. For example:

> Check out the chessboard. Chelsea is the champion.

## Creating Your Word List

**WORD BOX**

- chain
- chance
- chapter
- cherry
- Churchill
- bunch
- French
- kitchen
- peaches
- watched

**Say these words:**

cherry   bunch   chain   kitchen

What do these 4 words have in common?
All of the words have the **ch sound**.
What kind of sound is **ch** in these words? The **ch sound** is a "hard" sound.

**1.** Make a list of words that have the **ch sound**. Use the chants to help you. As you read the words out loud, STRESS the **ch sound**.

**2.** Work with your teacher to create the list of **ch** words you will be learning to spell.
You can use: the Word Box, the chants, your own words.
These are your Lesson Words.

**3. In your notebook**
- Write the Lesson Words and underline the **ch sound** in each word.
- You may want to add **ch** words to your Personal Dictionary List to help in your reading and writing.

## STRATEGY SPOT

### Find Related Words — Meaning Patterns

**Words that are similar, or related, in meaning often have similar spellings. By thinking about what the word means and its root word, you can begin to spell the word. Here are examples:**

1. Look at your Lesson Words.
2. Pick 3 words and "explode" them by writing other forms of the word. Do it like this:

**QUICK TIP**

Ch is a **digraph**. It can be at the beginning, middle, or end of a word. Sh is also a digraph. Make sure you pronounce the **sh** and **ch** sounds correctly.

# Zoom in on Your Words

1. **Charley Chant** Make a new chant by replacing the underlined words in the chant on page 64 with **ch** words. Your chant does not need to make sense.

2. **Scrunch Up** Print 6 of your Lesson Words, but do not leave any spaces between the words.
   Do it like this: **cherrychainbunch**
   Have your partner circle and read each Lesson Word.

3. **Stress It!** Read each of your Lesson Words and really STRESS the **ch** sound. Tap your finger on the desk as you say each **ch**.

4. **A Bunch of Cherries** Someone dropped a bunch of cherries. Match the cherry parts to make 5 **ch** words.

65

**5. Watch the Letter Ladder** Pick your longest Lesson Word. Write it in a column, from top to bottom. Use your other Lesson Words to fill in the ladder. Do it like this:

```
            w
    c h a i n
c h a p t e r
        c
    c h i e f
        e
        d
```

*cherry chicken*

**AT HOME**

**6. Chewy Foods from the Kitchen**
The names of many foods contain the **ch sound**. List the names of foods that are **ch** words. For example: **ch**erry, **ch**icken. If you need help, look in the kitchen! Find other **ch** words around your house.

**7. A Bunch of Disappearing Letters** Now you see them. Now you don't! With a partner, print each of your Lesson Words on a chalkboard or in your notebook. Softly say each letter, then erase it. After you have erased all the letters, try printing the word again from memory.

**8. One Peach, Two Peaches ...** When a word ends in **ch**, you have to add **-es** to make it plural (to mean more than one). Like this: peach – peach**es**.
Add **-es** to the following words to make them plural:
    a) watch      b) bunch      c) batch
    d) lunch      e) witch      f) match

**TRY THIS!** For an extra challenge, use 2 of these **-es** words in interesting sentences.

### DID YOU KNOW?
When we are learning to write, the first step is writing just the **consonants** of the words, and then we learn to include **vowels**.

## Focus on Language ▸ Joined Words — Compounds

A **compound word** is 2 smaller words joined to form 1 word. The 2 small words **make the meaning** of the compound word. For example:

back + ground = **background**
home + sick = **homesick**

**1.** Make compounds by joining a word from column **a)** with a word from column **b)**.

| a) | b) |
|---|---|
| wind | parent |
| rail | body |
| down | burger |
| home | road |
| every | sick |
| ham | shield |
| grand | stairs |

**2.** Pick 1 compound word from number **1** above. Draw 2 pictures to show the small words and a picture for the compound word.

**3.** Look at these pictures to find compound words.

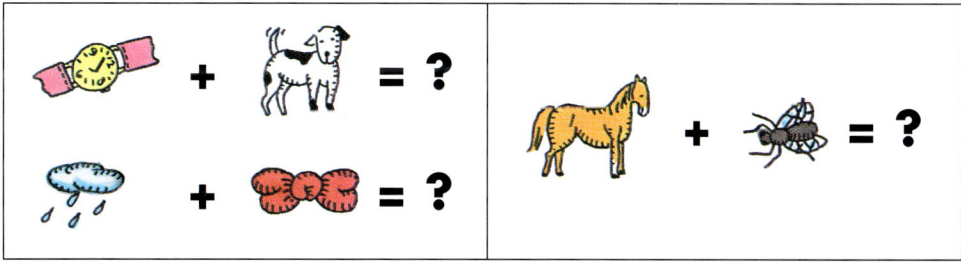

**4.** Think of other compound words and illustrate them with pictures as you did in number **2**.

### FLASHBACK

Look at your work from the beginning of the year — or even from last year. Tell 3 things that you have learned.

# 17 ough and Challenge Words

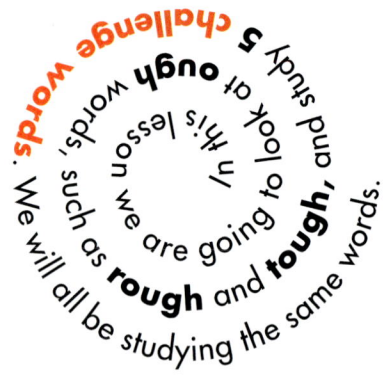

## Creating Your Word List

**WORD BOX**

rough
tough
enough
cough
roughly

**Say these words:**

What sound do these 3 words have?

1. As a class, make a list of words that have the **gh sound**. Which letters are silent, and what sound does **gh** make?

2. Write your Lesson Words:
   - Write down the 5 **ough** words from the Word Box.
   - Add these 5 *challenge words*:
     *course, told, were, because, heard*
   - Underline the silent letters in each word. These are your Lesson Words.

3. **In your notebook**
   - Highlight the parts of the words you find difficult.
   - Does any word in English begin with **gh**? What can you say about the place of **gh** in a word?
   - Keep adding **ough** words and *challenge words* to your Personal Dictionary List. Don't forget to keep it up to date.

# Zoom in on Your Words

1. **Get in Shape!** Draw the **wordprint** shape for each of these Lesson Words:

   a) enough   b) because   c) heard
   d) cough    e) were

2. **Word Pyramid** Choose a word you want to practise. Draw a triangle in your notebook. On the first line, print the first letter of the word. On the second line, print the first 2 letters. On the third line, the first 3 letters. Continue until the triangle is full. Do a pyramid with 2 other Lesson Words.

3. **Be a Word Artist!** Pick 5 Lesson Words and print them in fancy letters.

4. **Because** With a partner, make a 1-word poem. One person says the word **Because**. The second person responds by saying the word **Because** in a different tone of voice. Keep going back and forth changing your voice.
   **TRY THIS!** For an extra challenge, do this with another Lesson Word.

5. **What Can You Hear Here?** **Homophones** are words that sound the same but are spelled differently and have different meanings. The words **hear** and **here** are homophones.

   I am waiting for you **here**.
   I cannot **hear** the music.

   What little word is inside **hear** that will help you remember the difference between these 2 words? Write down the pair of homophones and draw a little picture beside each one. Add them to your class list of homophones.

## QUICK TIP

Our Lesson Words with **gh** have the "**ff**" sound, but in some words such as **bought**, **thought**, and **through** the **gh** is silent.

## STRATEGY SPOT

### Spelling Traps — Study Challenge Words

**Challenge Words** are words that are difficult to spell. They are not spelled the way they sound. Don't let a challenge word become a spelling trap for you! Use your spelling strategies to study and practise these words regularly.

AT HOME

6. **Sharing Challenge Word Strategies** Tell someone at home about some of the **challenge words** you have been studying. Share how you remember the spelling of these unusual or difficult words. Ask about the words that are challenge words for him or her.

7. **Complete the Sentences** Complete these sentences in your notebook.
   a) Of course you can …
   b) I told you …
   c) She was excited because …
   d) When I heard …
   e) We were …

8. **That Makes Me Think of …** Often one word makes us think of another. For example, if you say **tough**, many people will say **rough**. Play Word Association with a partner. Say a Lesson Word and have your partner say the first word or words that come to mind.

### FLASHBACK

**Challenge words** are not spelled the way they sound.
Think of 5 **challenge words** you can now spell.

# Connecting with MATH

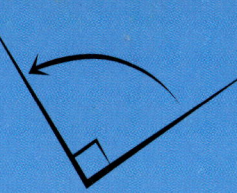

**Geometry** was first used by architects in ancient Greece to help them design buildings. Architects today have to study geometry so that their building designs are safe, are pleasing, and can be constructed.

**Look at the buildings in your community. What interesting shapes do you see? Make a list of shape words such as: rectangle, triangle, octagon. Use your spelling strategies to practise spelling these words.**

## Class Shape Booklet

**We are going to make a class shape booklet. Here's how:**

1. Choose a geometric shape and cut it out (rectangle, triangle, octagon, and so on). Your shape should be approximately 10 cm x 10 cm.

2. Write the name of the shape at the top of the shape. Using the letters in that shape's name, make as many words as you can. (You can mix up the order of the letters.) You can use both sides of your shape to list your words. **Proofread** your new words to check for spelling mistakes.

3. All students punch a hole in their shape. Thread a piece of yarn or heavy string through each hole. String the shapes all together and tie a knot. You now have a class shape booklet!

The next time you see a building being constructed, remember that an architect who studied geometry designed that building.

# 18 SPELL CHECK

## REVIEW

**Patterns**

nk
ck
-tion
ch
ough and challenge words

**Strategies**

1. Highlight letters that need attention.
2. Give it a go! — Leave a blank.
3. See it — Visualize words.
4. Find related words.
5. Spelling traps—Study challenge words

## Creating Your Word List

**In your notebook**
- Go to your list of "Words I Still Need to Practise."
- Pick 10 words you need to practise spelling.
- Beside each word, write the letters you need to focus on. Like this:

  direction – **ec**,  enough – **gh**

## Zoom in on Your Words

1. **Be a Slowpoke**  S...l...o...w...l...y say each word to yourself and listen to every sound in the word. Make sure you say each sound of the word.

2. **Wordprints**  Draw the wordprint of your Lesson Words. For example:

3. **Counting Syllables**  Pick 3 Lesson Words and count out the syllables in each word.

4. **Shrink It!**  Pick a Lesson Word and write it in a way that helps you understand the meaning. For example:

5. **Headlines Make News**  Create a headline using 1 of your Lesson Words. Do this 3 times to create 3 great headlines.

6. **Bumblebee** Play the Bumblebee game with a partner. Player A chooses a Lesson Word and writes down a dash for each letter of the word. Player B has to figure out the word by suggesting 1 letter at a time. Only 1 guess of the final word is allowed. For every incorrect guess, Player A draws another part of the Bumblebee. Then switch roles. Watch out for that stinger!

7. **String It Up** You will need white paper, yarn, and white glue for this activity. Lightly spell a **challenge word** or a Lesson Word in fancy printing on a piece of white paper. Put some white glue on the outline of the first letter and then place some yarn on the letter. Do the rest of the letters in the same way. Use different colours of yarn. Add a border.

AT HOME

8. **Study Your Spelling Words** Look at the Strategy Spot on page 25 in Lesson 5. Use some of the 6 study skills to practise your Lesson Words.

9. **A Collection of Sorts** Write each of your Lesson Words on small pieces of paper. Think of different ways to sort your words: Sort by meaning, sort by spelling pattern, sort by **vowel sound**.

10. **Down the Letter Ladder** Pick your longest Lesson Word. Write it in a column. Use your other Lesson Words to fill in the ladder. You can also use other words you know how to spell.

11. **Revisit Your Lesson Words** Pick 3 Lesson Words you need to practise and print them in fancy letters using coloured pencils.

## FLASHBACK

Look at the Lesson Words you now know how to spell. Cross them off your list of "Words I Still Need to Practise." Bravo! You're becoming a spelling superstar.

# Hard and Soft c

Remember this ice cream rhyme?

> I scream.
> You scream.
> We all scream
> For ice cream!

## Creating Your Word List

**WORD BOX**

- dance
- cutting
- since
- magic
- police
- coast
- cities
- cemetery
- canary
- cannot
- space

**Say these words:**

face   cent   place

What sound is made by the letter **c**? This is called a **soft c**.

**Say these words:**

cage   coin   camp

What sound is made by the letter **c**? This is called a **hard c**.

**Now say these words:**

climb   magic   crash   city   race

Put the words into a chart like this:

| hard c | soft c |
|--------|--------|
|        |        |

1. As a class, make a list of words that have either a **hard c sound** or a **soft c sound**. Add your words to the chart.

2. Work with your teacher to create the list of **hard** and **soft c** words you will be learning to spell.
   You can use: the Word Box, the rhyme, your own words.
   These are your Lesson Words.

## STRATEGY SPOT — Proofreading — Scan Back!

Here's a proofreading tip. Read your work backwards! This way you will pay attention to the spelling of each word instead of the meaning of what you have written. To proofread the sentence "My friend cannot meet me at the movies," you would read the words in this order: movies the at me meet cannot friend My.

# Zoom in on Your Words

1. **Words in Words**  Find smaller words in as many of the Lesson Words as you can. Draw a circle around them.

2. **Scrunched-up Words**  Print 8 of your Lesson Words without leaving spaces between the words. See if your partner can find the 8 words.

3. **Wordprints**  A footprint shows the shape of a foot. A **wordprint** shows the shape of a word. Draw the wordprint shape for each of these words:
   - a) cutting
   - b) police
   - c) cannot
   - d) canary
   - e) since
   - f) dance
   - g) space
   - h) coast

4. **I Sent a Cent — Homophones**

   The kitchen was filled with the scent of baking bread.
   Mother sent me to the store to buy milk.
   I need one more cent to make a dollar.

   Write down the 3 **homophones** in the sentences above and draw little pictures to show the meaning of each word. Add the words to your class list of homophones. Come up with 3 sentences on your own.

**QUICK TIP**

Words that start with **ci** or **ce** are pronounced with an **s** sound.

5. **Ice Cream Scoops** Scoop the syllables in the different flavours of ice cream to make Word Box words.

6. **Scan Back!** Help Caitlin proofread her **hard** and **soft c** words. Start at the END of the paragraph.

   My best kind of ise cream is vanilla. Ise cream is nise and kold on a hot summer day. I kannot be without my ise cream.

   Copy the paragraph correctly in your notebook.

7. **Shorten Up** The word **cannot** can be shortened to **can't**. Write the shortened words for the following.
   - a) did not
   - b) she will
   - c) they are
   - d) have not
   - e) I have
   - f) you had

   **TRY THIS!** For an extra challenge, use 2 of your new words in interesting sentences. Don't forget to **proofread**!

8. **Word Association** Often one word makes us think of another. For example, if you say the word **canary**, many people will say **yellow**. Play Word Association with a partner. Say a Lesson Word and have the person say the first word or words that come to mind.

AT HOME

9. **And the Winner Is ...** Did you know that the all-time favourite flavour of ice cream is vanilla? Is there ice cream in your freezer? What kind? Ask everyone in your house what his or her favourite ice cream flavour is. Share your findings with the class.

## FLASHBACK

What strategy do you use to spell **hard** and **soft c** words?

# Connecting with Art

## The Creative Shape of Words

1. Write any 4 of these words in a shape that gives a clue to their meaning:

   spring, tree, smoke, escalator, boomerang,
   doughnut, sunshine, umbrella, toothbrush

2. Pick your best one. Have fun! Use crayons, markers, coloured pencils, or paint to describe the word in a colourful way. You may wish to use a computer to create your word picture.

3. Use the pictures to make a class bulletin board. You may want to add some of the words to your Personal Dictionary List.

What other words can you illustrate in a special way to show their meaning?

# 20 igh, eigh

Have you seen notices like these? Where have you seen them?

## Creating Your Word List

**Say these words:**

What 2 **long vowel sounds** do these words have?

**WORD BOX**

height
frightened
daylight
tonight
sight
highway
sigh
eight
weigh
right

1. Make a list of words that have the spelling patterns **igh** and **eigh**. Use the notices at the top of this page to help you. As you read each word in the list out loud, STRESS the **long vowel sound**.

2. Work with your teacher to create the list of **igh** or **eigh** words you will be learning to spell.
   You can use: the Word Box, the notices, your own words. These are your Lesson Words.

3. **In your notebook**
   - Write the Lesson Words and circle the **igh** or **eigh** pattern in each word.
   - You may want to add some of these words to your Personal Dictionary List.

## STRATEGY SPOT

### I Know That Pattern! — Word Families

Word families help you to spell new words. You know how to spell **light**, and by rhyming the word and following the pattern you can now spell **bright**, **night**, and **flight**.

# Zoom in on Your Words

1. **Underline It!** Write these sentences in your notebook and underline the words with the sound of **long i**.
   a) Monica was not frightened by the height of the roller-coaster ride.
   b) The river ran high after the rainstorm.
   c) I need new pants: mine are too tight!
   d) We will travel the highway during daylight.

2. **Word Search** Write the Lesson Words you find in the puzzle in your notebook.

| h | s | i | y | o | q | h | z | y | a | n | t | n | u |
| w | e | i | d | e | n | e | t | h | g | i | r | f | f |
| m | h | i | g | q | f | n | p | h | n | w | f | r | k |
| i | s | r | g | h | h | n | q | t | l | c | y | r | q |
| i | c | i | p | h | t | h | o | w | w | j | q | p | e |
| z | t | y | g | l | t | n | i | h | r | c | f | i | v |
| l | h | n | y | h | i | a | k | g | t | t | g | h | a |
| l | g | y | z | g | b | y | t | u | h | h | k | u | m |
| d | i | n | h | n | z | p | a | g | t | w | h | o | p |
| e | r | t | o | v | u | h | i | j | x | g | a | g | k |
| b | c | k | f | v | w | l | j | d | i | h | w | y | w |
| a | e | z | a | g | y | w | p | e | m | g | v | o | p |
| n | z | h | l | a | v | q | w | g | r | f | a | f | g |
| y | x | q | d | w | v | h | n | r | s | e | l | v | n |

**TRY THIS!** For an extra challenge, make your own Word Search to share with a partner.

79

3. **Can't Fool Me!** Not all words that rhyme have the same spelling pattern. For example: **white**, **night**.
   Choose words from the clouds to complete these sentences.
   - a) _____ is a time of darkness.
   - b) A frightened dog may _____ .
   - c) A _____ can fly in the wind.
   - d) The sun gives us heat and _____ .
   - e) A zebra is black and _____ .

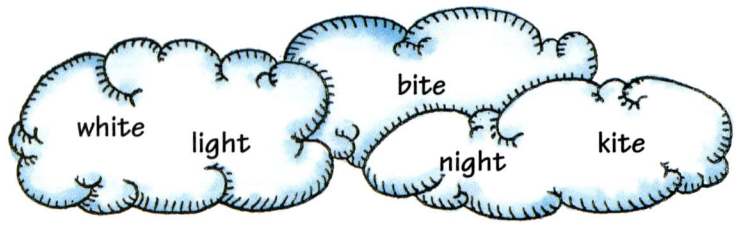

4. **Dictionary Please** Play "Dictionary Please" with a partner. One checks for the **-ite** pattern and the other for the **-ight** pattern to find the correct spelling for each word pair.
   - a) slite/slight
   - b) spite/spight
   - c) rite/right
   - d) site/sight
   - e) fight/fite
   - f) brite/bright.
   
   In which word pairs are BOTH spellings correct?

### DID YOU KNOW?
Some words sound like the action they describe. For example, say these words quickly: **ring**, **sneeze**, **boom**. Did you notice that what you said was the same as the sound?

AT HOME

5. **Create Words Tonight!** How many words can you make using the letters in each of these words:
   - a) frightened
   - b) daylight
   - c) height
   
   **TRY THIS!** For an extra challenge, choose a word of your own to make new words.

## FLASHBACK

What have you noticed about **igh** spelling patterns?

# Connecting with TECHNOLOGY

## Computer Spell Checks

A **spell check** on the computer will not solve ALL of your spelling problems. However, the spell check feature does many things:

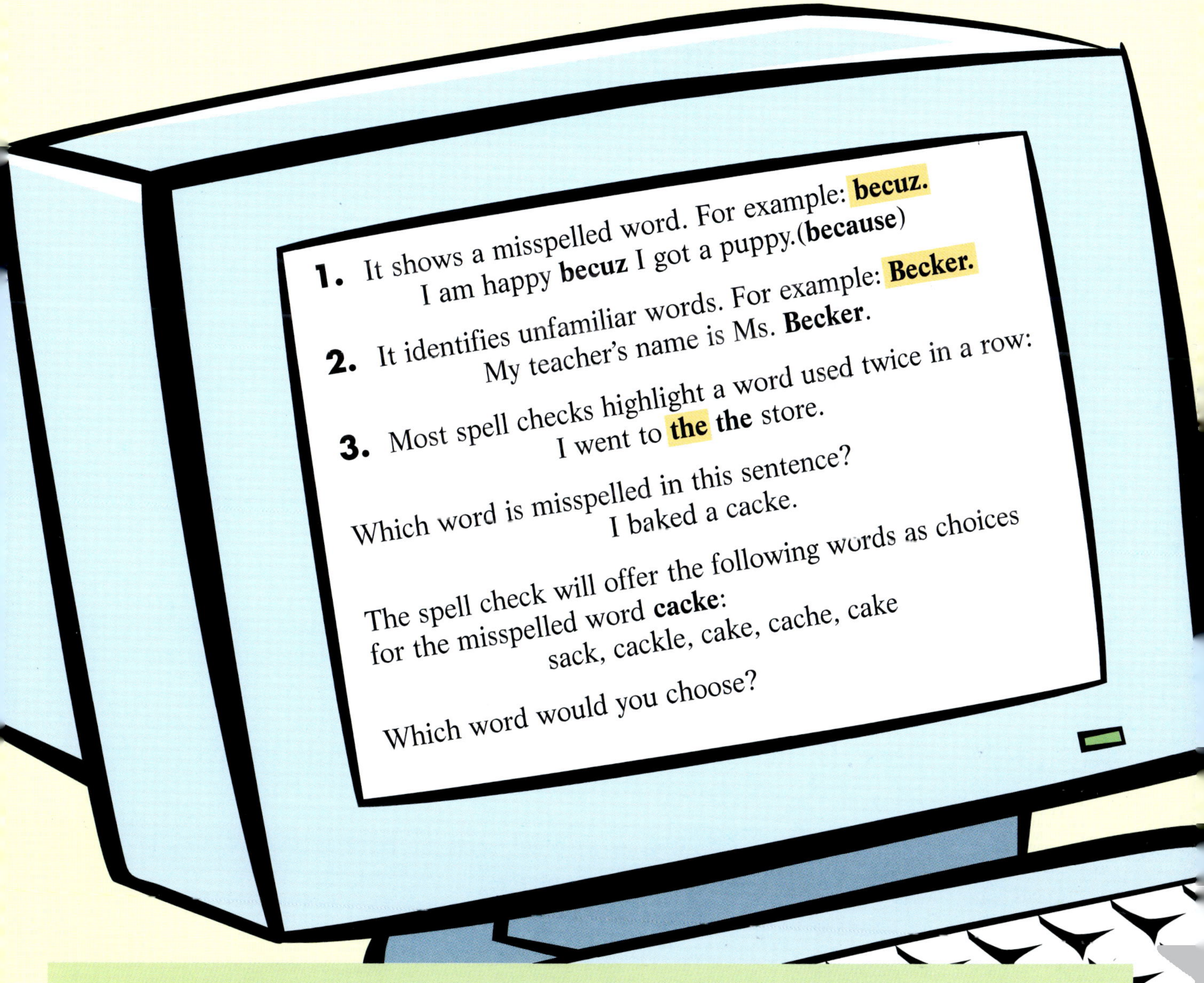

1. It shows a misspelled word. For example: **becuz**.
   I am happy **becuz** I got a puppy. (**because**)

2. It identifies unfamiliar words. For example: **Becker**.
   My teacher's name is Ms. **Becker**.

3. Most spell checks highlight a word used twice in a row:
   I went to **the the** store.

Which word is misspelled in this sentence?
I baked a cacke.

The spell check will offer the following words as choices for the misspelled word **cacke**:
sack, cackle, cake, cache, cake

Which word would you choose?

If you have a computer in your class, find out how the **spell check** works. Teach a partner how to use it. Write your next story on the computer, and use the spell check to help you **proofread**.

# 21 ph

Have fun reading this poem about a run-in between an elephant and a telephone.

### Eletelephony

Once there was an elephant,
Who tried to use the telephant —
No! no! I mean an elephone
Who tried to use the telephone —
(Dear me! I am not certain quite
That even now I've got it right.)
Howe'er it was, he got his trunk
Entangled in the telephunk;
The more he tried to get it free,
The louder buzzed the telephee —
(I fear I'd better drop the song
Of elephop and telephong!)

— Laura E. Richards

# Creating Your Word List

**WORD BOX**

telephone
nephew
gopher
graph
pharmacy
trophy
physical
photograph
elephant
alphabet

**Say these words:**

phone   photo   phrase

What sound do these words share? Which 2 letters produce the sound?

1. Make a class list of words that have the **ph sound**. As you read each word in the list out loud, STRESS the **ph sound**.

2. Work with your teacher to create the list of **ph** words you will be learning to spell.
   You can use: the Word Box, the poem, your own words.
   These are your Lesson Words.

**3. In your notebook**
- Write the Lesson Words and underline the **ph sound**.
- Keep adding **ph** words and **challenge words** to your Personal Dictionary List.

**STRATEGY SPOT**

**Proofreading — Read Out Loud**

When you are proofreading your work, read it out loud softly to yourself. You'll **hear** and **see** your spelling mistakes, missed words, and punctuation problems.

# Zoom in on Your Words

1. **Finish It** Use the Word Box to complete these sentences in your notebook.
   a) There are 26 letters in the _____ .
   b) In math, we made a _____ of our findings.
   c) Sean's soccer team won the _____ .
   d) My Aunt Maria has three nieces and one _____ .

   Read each sentence out loud to be sure you wrote it correctly.

2. **Scrambled Syllables** The gopher chewed up the telephone message. Unscramble the **syllables** to make **ph** words.
   a) phone e tel   b) phy tro   c) ma phar cy
   d) to graph pho   e) bet al pha

3. **Word Pyramid** Choose a word you want to practise. Draw a triangle. On the first line, print the first letter of the word. On the second line, print the first 2 letters. On the third line, the first 3 letters. Continue until the triangle is full. Do a pyramid with 2 other Lesson Words.

**DID YOU KNOW?**

**Gopher** is the name of a system that finds information on the worldwide computer Internet. Like the busy little animal, Gopher quickly gathers information and places it in sites called **gopher holes**.

**4. Word Stairs** Write down a Lesson Word or other word you can spell. Your partner or group uses the last letter of the word to start the next word. Take turns to see how far down you can make the stairs go. Do it like this:

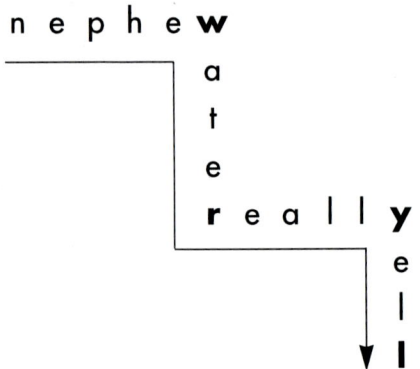

**QUICK TIP**

The sound **"f"** can be spelled using the letters **f**, **ph**, **gh**, **ff**, **lf**. Only the letter **f** or spelling pattern **ph** are used at the beginning of a word.

**5. f or ph?** Help Philip fill in the missing **f** or **ph** to complete these words. The clues will help you. Write the words in your notebook.
   a) a picture            __ otograph
   b) 4 x 10 =            __ orty
   c) a bird            __ easa**n**t
   d) a story with a lesson    __ able
   e) a pesky insect      __ **l**y

**TRY THIS!** For an extra challenge, add **ph** to the blue letters to spell a word that means "not real."

**6. Tele-photo-graph** The word part **tele** means "over a distance." **Photo** means "light" and **graph** means "something written or drawn."
Copy the words and underline the word parts in each:
   a) photograph    b) photocopy    c) autograph
   d) telephoto      e) television     f) telephone

**TRY THIS!** For an extra challenge, use 3 of the words in sentences that show their meaning. Proofread your sentences by reading them out loud.

**7. ph Hunt** Many of the **ph** words in the poem on page 82 are make-believe words. Find them.

**TRY THIS!** For an extra challenge, write your own funny poem using real and made-up **ph** words.

## Focus on Language — Opposites — Antonyms

When 2 words are opposite in meaning, they are called **antonyms**. For example:

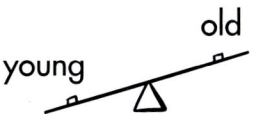 

1. Identify the word pairs in each sentence that are opposites:
   a) The cat kept coming in and out of the house.
   b) May I have a full box of juice? This one is empty.
   c) In the desert, hot days are followed by cold nights.

2. Some words can be made into antonyms by adding a **prefix** (for example: **un-**, **dis-**, **mis-**) to the beginning of the word. Like this: honest/**dis**honest, use/**mis**use.
   Pick the correct prefix and make the words opposite.

   | | |
   |---|---|
   | **un** | behave |
   | | obey |
   | **dis** | tidy |
   | | believe |
   | **mis** | kind |

**AT HOME**

3. **Family Photographs** Ask at home if there are any **photographs** of your family. If there are no photos, draw a family picture. Write an interesting story that tells about the photograph or your drawing. Remember to **proofread**!

4. Write a list of **antonyms** (opposites). Try for 10 pairs. Share your list with a partner.

## FLASHBACK

Remember: the **ph** pattern usually says "f." Which **ph** word did you add to your Personal Dictionary List?

# 22  ou

Try this chant!

Shout! Shout!
Shout it out loud.
Shout for the <u>doctor</u>,
Shout for the <u>baker</u>,
Shout for the <u>grocer</u>,
Shout for my <u>brother</u>,
Please bring me my <u>tea</u>.

## Creating Your Word List

**WORD BOX**

- country
- couple
- cousin
- hours
- proud
- sound
- couch
- doubt
- scout
- shout

**Say these words:**

sound   scout   bounce

What sound is made by the **ou pattern**?
If you were going to spell this pattern the way it sounds in these words, how would you spell it?

**Now say these words:**

What sound is made by the **ou** in these words?
In these words **ou** has the sound of **short u**.

1. Make a list of words that have the **ou pattern**. Use the chant to help you. As you read the words out loud, STRESS the **ou**.

2. Work with your teacher to create the list of **ou** words you will be learning to spell.
   You can use: the Word Box, the chant, words from your story writing or a theme your class is studying.

3. **In your notebook**
   - Write the Lesson Words and underline the **ou pattern** in each word.
   - Count the number of **syllables** in each Lesson Word.
   - Add **ou** words to your Personal Dictionary List.

## STRATEGY SPOT: Make an Acrostic

An **acrostic** is a word pattern that helps you remember. For example:

ROUGH     **R**ain
             **O**n
             **U**ncle
             **G**ordon's
             **H**ay

**Making up an acrostic and memorizing it helps you remember all of the letters in a word. Here is how you do it:**

1. Pick a word you want to learn to spell. Print it in a column, from top to bottom.
2. Write a word for each letter. It helps if the words almost make a sentence.
3. Pick a Lesson Word that is difficult for you and try out this spelling strategy.
4. Read a partner's acrostic.

**QUICK TIP**

The **ou pattern** can also have the sound of **long o** (m**ou**ld, sh**ou**lder) and **short o** (c**ou**gh, tr**ou**gh).

# Zoom in on Your Words

1. **Underline It!** Write Lesson Words that you need to practise. Underline the part of the word that needs extra attention. Use these words in sentences.

2. **Scrambled Words** Unscramble these words. Look in the Word Box if you need help.
   - a) oucelp
   - b) dourp
   - c) osutc
   - d) unods
   - e) scniuo
   - f) tubdo

3. **Shout!** What other words can you make from the letters in the word **shout**?

**AT HOME**

4. **Shout It Out!** Copy out the chant at the top of page 86. Leave the first 2 lines the same. Change the underlined words to new words. Read your chant out loud, with lots of enthusiasm!

5. **Foldover** Pick a Lesson Word you want to practise. See page 43 in Lesson 10 for detailed instructions on how to do a **foldover**.

6. **Counting on a Crossword** Use the clues to solve this **ou** crossword. The Lesson Words will help you.

**Across**
4 there are 24 in a day
6 to add numbers
7 16 make a pound (about 28 g)
9 2 sofas

**Down**
1 bigger than a hill
2 I _____ something for $25
3 what a basketball does
5 to yell
8 two

7. **Figure It Out** Copy the letter into your notebook and fill in the missing letters to figure out this message.

D _ ar Clas _ ,
I am ve_ y pr_ _ d of _ ou I dou _ t ther_ is a _ ot _ er class l _ ke o _ rs. W _ en I l _ _ k at yo _ r succ _ ss with spe _ _ ing, I kn _ w h _ w h _ rd you ha _ _ w _ rk _ d. We h _ ve spe _ t h _ _ rs studyin _ p _ tter _ s and str_ t _ gies. _ e now kno _ many s _ _ nds and s _ elli _ gs. In a cou _ _ e of mon _ hs, we have m _ de progress. So _ _ out out h _ _ ray for our gr _ de _ our cla _ s!

88

> **DID YOU KNOW?**
> Reading and writing help you to become a better speller. The more you work with and enjoy words, the more you are learning about the way the English language works.

## Focus on Language  Naming Words — Nouns

A **noun** is a naming word. We use a noun to name a **person**, a **place**, a **thing**, a **feeling**, and an **idea**.

| | |
|---|---|
| person | **woman, doctor** … |
| place | **school, Vancouver** … |
| thing | **bicycle, computer** … |
| feeling | **happiness, fear** … |
| idea | **peace, belief** … |

1. Make a chart of nouns. Sort them by **person**, **place**, **thing**, **feeling**, and **idea**.

2. In a small group, play the game "I packed my suitcase with a…." Each player completes the sentence by naming an object. Your word must start with the last letter of the word given by the last player. For example:
   I packed my suitcase with a **zebra**.
   I packed my suitcase with an **alligator**.
   I packed my suitcase with a **radio**.
   All of these words are **nouns**.

3. Read over the story in Connecting with Literature on page 23 in Lesson 4. Find 5 **nouns** in the story. Use 3 of these nouns in interesting sentences. Remember to **proofread** your work.

### FLASHBACK

Reread number 7 in Zoom in on Your Words on page 88. Think of all the things that you have learned in spelling this year.

# 23 Hard and Soft g

Let's look at some **g** words from the dictionary. Notice all the things the dictionary tells us about each word:

**gallop** (gal´ əp) *v.* (for a horse) to run at full speed: *The horse galloped across the bridge.*

**gentle** (jen´ təl) *adj.* **1.** soft; low: *a gentle voice.* **2.** mild; not rough: *a gentle breeze.*

**giant** (ji´ ənt) *n.* an imaginary person of huge size and great strength: *The giant's goose lay golden eggs.*

**gutter** (gut´ ər) *n.* a channel for carrying off overflowing water: *The gutter was attached to the edge of the garage roof.*

## Creating Your Word List

**WORD BOX**

- gallop
- giant
- gentle
- garage
- goose
- glove
- guess
- bridge
- edge
- greatest

**Say these words:**

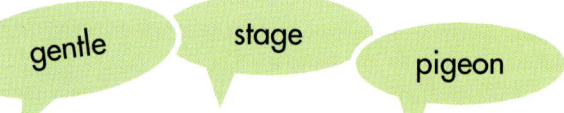

gentle, stage, pigeon

What sound is made by the letter **g**? This is called a **soft g**.

**Say these words:**

game, gold, grade

What sound is made by the letter **g**? This is called a **hard g**.

**Now say these words:**

gym, goat, ridge, grow, strange

Notice the sound of the letter **g** in each word.

1. Make a list of words that have either a **hard g** or a **soft g**. Use the dictionary entries to help you.

2. Work with your teacher to create the list of **hard** and **soft g** words you will be learning to spell.
   You can use: the Word Box, the dictionary entries, your own words.

3. **In your notebook**
   - Write the Lesson Words. Underline each **hard g** and **soft g sound**.
   - Keep adding **hard g** and **soft g** words to your Personal Dictionary List. Don't forget to keep it up to date.

## STRATEGY SPOT — Proofreading — Share It!

Sometimes it is difficult to find the spelling mistakes in your own work. Ask a partner to proofread your work with you. By reading aloud together, you'll spot the spelling mistakes a lot faster.

# Zoom in on Your Words

1. **Circles/Boxes** Write the following words. Draw a **circle** around each **soft g** and a **box** around each **hard g sound**. Copy the words into your notebook.
   - a) garage
   - b) goose
   - c) gentle
   - d) bridge
   - e) giant
   - f) gallop

2. **Finish It** Use the Word Box to complete these sentences in your notebook.
   - a) The pony began to _____ when it heard the loud noise.
   - b) I had to _____ the answer because I wasn't sure.
   - c) Gina lost a _____ when she went skiing.
   - d) Sami was fishing over the _____ of the _____ .

91

> **DID YOU KNOW?**
> **Zippers** got their name from the sound they make when you **zip** them up or down. Listen carefully the next time you use a zipper.

3. **Giant Letter Ladder** Pick your longest Lesson Word. Write it in a column, from top to bottom. Use other Lesson Words to fill in the ladder. You can also use other words you know how to spell. Like this:

```
                g
        b  r  i  d  g  e
              g  a  m  e
     g  r  o  w  n
     g  a  t  e
```

**QUICK TIP**

The letter **j** often sounds like a **soft g**. Use a dictionary when in doubt!

4. **All Sorts of Animals** In a group, make a list of animals that start with the letter **g**. Sort the words into groups based on **hard** or **soft g**.

   **TRY THIS!** For an extra challenge, write a short paragraph about 1 of the animals you listed. Ask a partner to **proofread** your work with you, reading it out loud.

5. **g or j?** Use a **g** or a **j** to complete each word. The clues will help you.

   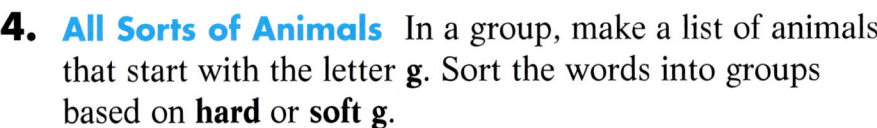
   a) a prison                         _ ail
   b) an orange-coloured cat           _ inger
   c) a bird found in the city         pi _ eon
   d) a long-necked animal             _ iraffe
   e) to hop up                        _ ump

   When you are done, add **g** or **j** to the blue letters to spell something that can make you sick.

6. **Just a Little Bit** Instead of saying **gymnasium**, we shorten the word to **gym**. Write each of the following words and the shortened word we can use.

   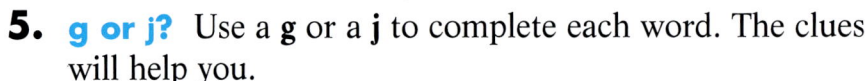
   a) submarine     b) airplane       c) photograph
   d) chimpanzee    e) veterinarian   f) telephone

**AT HOME**

**7. Headline Hunt!** Look at the headlines in a newspaper or magazine. Cut out or copy 5 headlines and bring them to class tomorrow. In class, discuss the key words in the headlines.

# Focus on Language ▶ Dictionary Skills

One way to find words quickly in the dictionary is to use the 2 **guide words** at the top of each page. The first guide word tells you the first word on the dictionary page. The other guide word is the last entry word.

| gash | ▶ | geography |

**1.** Let's practise. Choose the pair of **guide words** that would be at the top of the dictionary page where you would find the word **leopard**:
  a) lever — light
  b) legend — level
  c) later — lean

**2.** Use your dictionary and write the 2 guide words at the top of the page where each of these words is found:
  a) edge    b) giant    c) guess
  d) bridge  e) art      f) chart

**3.** Find 3 interesting words in the dictionary. See if your partner can find them in the dictionary using the guide words to help.

## FLASHBACK

Look over all of the activities in this lesson. Which one helped you the most?

# 24 SPELL CHECK

## REVIEW

**Patterns**

hard and soft c
igh, eigh
ph
ou
hard and soft g

**Strategies**

1. Proofreading — Scan back!
2. I know that pattern! — Word families.
3. Proofreading — Read out loud.
4. Make an acrostic
5. Proofreading — Share it!

## Creating Your Word List

**In your notebook**
- Go to your list of "Words I Still Need to Practise."
- Pick 10 words you need to practise spelling.

## Zoom in on Your Words

1. **Slowpoke** S...l...o...w...l...y say each word to yourself. Listen to every sound in the word.

2. **Circle It** Draw a circle around the part of the word you need to focus on.

3. **Snap, Clap, Tap** Pick 3 Lesson Words and snap, clap, or tap out the **syllables** in each word.

4. **Alphaspell** Play Alphaspell with a partner. Write down any 3 letters of the alphabet. Your partner thinks up words for the letters. Like this:

   **CDT** – Cannot Dance Tonight

   Take turns giving each other alphabet letters.

   **TRY THIS!** For an extra challenge, use extra alphabet letters!

5. **All Sorts of Words** Write each of your Lesson Words on small pieces of paper. Think of different ways to sort your words: Sort by meaning, sort by spelling pattern, sort by **consonant sound**.

6. **Come One, Come All!** Make a poster to announce a Kids Day celebration. On your poster, be sure to give this important information about your event:

    time, location, entertainment, food, prizes, activities, admission charge

7. **Word Web** Say the word **telephone**. What 2 other words come to mind? Complete a Word Web using as many words as you can.

8. **Proof It!** Pick 1 of the following strategies:
    a) Proofreading — Scan back!
    b) I know that pattern! — Word families
    c) Proofreading — Read out loud

    Use that strategy to **proofread** a story you wrote this week.

9. **Down the Word Stairs** Write down a Lesson Word or other word you can spell. Have a partner use the last letter of the word to start a new word. Take turns and see how far down you can make the stairs go.

10. **Study Your Spelling Words** Look at the Strategy Spot on page 25 in Lesson 5. Use some of the 6 study skills to practise your Lesson Words.

## FLASHBACK

Look at the Lesson Words that you now know how to spell. Cross them off your list of "Words I Still Need to Practise." Congratulations! You're a real spelling champion.

# 25 ir, or, ur

Enjoy this poem. But let's hope this never happens to YOU!

**The Apple and the Worm**

I bit an apple
   That had a worm.
I swallowed the apple,
   I swallowed the worm.
I felt it squiggle,
   I felt it squirm.
I felt it wiggle,
   I felt it turn …

I guess that worm is there to stay
Unless …
I swallow a bird some day!

— Robert Heidbreder

## Creating Your Word List

**WORD BOX**

- turtle
- birch
- world
- squirrel
- third
- curve
- author
- circus
- motor
- nurse

**Say these words:**

burst   word   skirt

What sound do these 3 words have in common?
Can you hear the **sound** of "**er**" in these words?

1. As a class, make a list of words that have the "**er**" **sound**. Use the poem "The Apple and the Worm" to help you. Put the words into a chart like this:

| ir | or | ur |
|----|----|----|
|    |    |    |

2. Work with your teacher to create the list of Lesson Words that have the "**er**" **sound**.
   You can use: the Word Box, the poem, your own words.

3. **In your notebook**
   - Write the Lesson Words. Circle the letters that make the **sound** of "**er**."
   - Add new **ir**, **or**, and **ur** words that you find in your reading and writing to your Personal Dictionary List.

### STRATEGY SPOT

### Pronounce Words Clearly!

Sometimes we do not spell words correctly because we are not saying them clearly. **Pronouncing** words carefully will help you with their spelling. Say these words:

Feb**r**uary, ar**c**tic, lib**r**ary, Wed**n**esday, vale**n**tine

Be sure to say each of your Lesson Words carefully when writing them down.

# Zoom in on Your Words

1. **Circle It!** Copy the Lesson Words, circling the **or**, **ur**, or **ir**.

2. **Missing Letters** The computer keyboard keeps sticking! Help fill in the missing letters to make Lesson Words.
   - a) w _ _ m
   - b) c _ _ ve
   - c) mot _ _
   - d) t _ _ tle
   - e) th _ _ d
   - f) c _ _ cus

3. **Finish It!** Use the Word Box to help you complete these sentences.
   - a) Bring some nuts to feed the _____ in the park.
   - b) The _____ of October is my birthday.
   - c) Never pull the bark from a _____ tree.
   - d) Robert Munsch is a well-known _____ of children's books.

### DID YOU KNOW?

Sayings constantly come and go in our language. Years ago, people used terms such as **groovy** or the **cat's pyjamas** to describe something they liked. Nowadays, we might use **cool** or **radical**!

## QUICK TIP

The sound "**e + r**" can be spelled **er**, **or**, **ir**, or **ur**. The **er** pattern is often found at the end of words.

**4. What Do You Do?** We can add **-or** to some words to make the names of occupations (what people do). Like this:

    **act** – An act**or** is a person who acts.

Add **-or** to these words to make new words:
- **a)** visit
- **b)** instruct
- **c)** sail
- **d)** contract
- **e)** direct
- **f)** edit
- **g)** collect
- **h)** conduct

Use your spelling strategies to learn these new words.

**5. Word Search** Write the **ir**, **or**, and **ur** words from the puzzle into your notebook.

| y | c | n | t | t | r | i | d | h | z | h | a | f | b |
|---|---|---|---|---|---|---|---|---|---|---|---|---|---|
| u | w | u | z | r | b | k | o | l | c | v | g | b | r |
| n | h | s | g | g | i | x | m | r | i | d | e | a | e |
| e | s | f | u | r | r | k | u | y | v | s | v | l | g |
| i | j | q | b | c | g | h | s | v | i | j | r | n | b |
| e | s | t | u | k | c | t | p | r | a | o | y | f | n |
| f | p | u | o | i | b | h | p | k | t | r | u | i | g |
| w | o | r | a | n | r | r | r | i | r | w | t | i | l |
| h | r | k | k | e | u | r | s | x | q | m | l | a | n |
| a | t | e | p | s | f | i | e | t | u | r | t | l | e |
| r | c | y | r | r | v | o | p | l | e | y | n | i | d |

**TRY THIS!** For an extra challenge, make up your own Word Search for a partner.

**6. Word Web** Authors use **Word Webs** to help with their stories. Copy this Word Web and complete it using your own words.

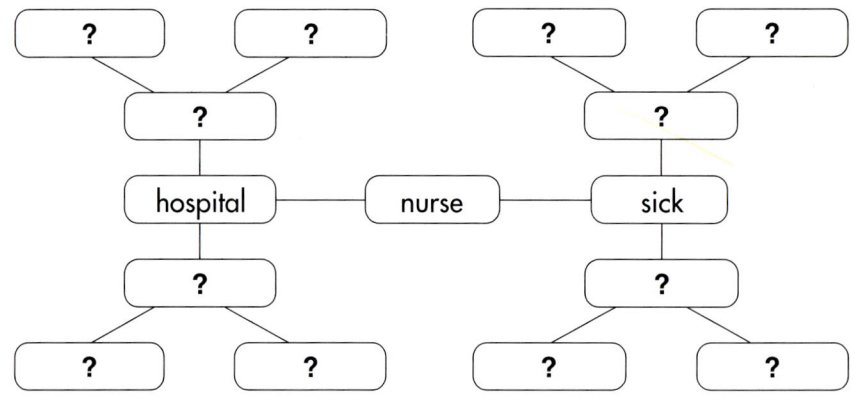

98

**7. Scrambled Words** Unscramble the "**er**" word to match each clue.

| | | |
|---|---|---|
| a) | a colour | pleurp |
| b) | helps you get well | tocdor |
| c) | to spin | nrut |
| d) | after twenty-nine | yitrht |
| e) | a bird sound | rphci |

**TRY THIS!** For an extra challenge, make clues for 5 Lesson Words to share with a partner.

# Focus on Language ▶ Alliteration

**Alliteration** is the use of the same sound at the beginning of several words. Alliteration is used in tongue twisters:

**P**eter **P**iper **p**icked a **p**eck of **p**ickled **p**eppers.

**Alliteration** is used in poems and books. For example, Shel Silverstein wrote a poem about **S**arah **C**ynthia **S**ylvia **S**tout. Author-illustrator Graeme Base used alliteration in *Animalia* to describe animals. Like this:

**P**roud **P**eacocks **P**reening **P**erfect **P**lumage

**A Lot of Alliterations** On your way home, look at the things around you. Try to make an **alliteration** for **school bus**. Like this:

**S**ix **s**hiny **s**chool **b**uses **s**tart **s**lowly **s**outhward.

Write 3 more alliterations for things you notice on the way home. Use your **proofreading** strategies to check your spelling. Share your alliterations with someone at home.

## FLASHBACK

Have you noticed how much more clearly you are **pronouncing** your words? Tongue twisters are a good way to practise your speaking skills.

# 26 pr- and ex-

Extra! Extra! Read all about it!

>Extra! Extra! Read all about it!
>Proper spelling is number 1.
>
>Extra! Extra! Read all about it!
>Practice makes perfect.
>
>Extra! Extra! Read all about it!
>Excellent at spelling, and proud of it!

## Creating Your Word List

1. Make a list of words that start with **pr-** and **ex-**. Use the newspaper banners to help you get started.
   As you read each word in the list out loud, STRESS the **pr-** or **ex- sound**.

2. Work with your teacher to create the list of **pr-** and **ex-** words you will be learning to spell.
   You can use: the Word Box, the banners, your own words. These are your Lesson Words.

3. **In your notebook**
   - Write each Lesson Word and <u>underline</u> the part that you need to practise.
   - Say each word to yourself and imagine the word in your mind.
   - You may want to add some of these words to your Personal Dictionary List.

**WORD BOX**

produce
prize
proper
promise
present
exercise
except
example
explosion
Prince Edward Island

# Zoom in on Your Words

1. **Crossword Time** Find your Lesson Words and write them in your notebook.

**Across**
3 an activity to build the body
4 a Canadian province
5 a loud noise

**Down**
1 another word for gift
2 what the winner gets

2. **Scrambled Words** Rena dropped the Word Box! Unscramble the words and copy them into your notebook.

lxpesooin
irmepos
eepaxml
cdoerpu

**TRY THIS!** For an extra challenge, unscramble the letters in the circles to spell a Word Box word that tells something you do in the gym.

## STRATEGY SPOT: Build Word Families by Sound

Sometimes if we can spell one word, we can spell another. Some of your Lesson Words have the **pr- sound**. This is a **consonant sound family**.

1. Identify the **consonant sound families** in these groups of words.
   a) prize, proof, problem, print
   b) wishes, shark, splash, shower

2. Look through your speller to find other sound families for **consonants**.

### DID YOU KNOW?
The word **quay** (a dock where boats unload) is pronounced "**key**." What ideas do you have for remembering how to spell and pronounce this challenge word?

3. **Find the Right One!** **Proofread** for spelling. Copy the words into your notebook and <u>underline</u> the correctly spelled word in each row.
   a) laf, laugh, laph
   b) oshun, ocun, ocean
   c) wich, whic, witch
   d) people, peeple, pepul

4. **Don't Be Fooled!** Complete the following words using **pr-**, **per-**, or **pur-**.
   a) a handbag      _ _ _ se
   b) maybe          _ _ _ haps
   c) a salty snack  _ _ etzel
   d) sweat          _ _ _ spiration

   Use your spelling strategies to learn these words.

AT HOME

5. **Canada Our Country** What makes your part of Canada special? Complete this sentence 5 times: **Canada is …**

6. **Alphaspell** Play Alphaspell with a partner. Write down any 3 letters of the alphabet. Your partner thinks up words for the letters. Like this:

   **TMZ** — Terry's Marvellous Zebra

   Take turns giving each other alphabet letters and solutions.
   **TRY THIS!** For an extra challenge, use 4 alphabet letters!

## FLASHBACK

Tell a partner about one of your favourite spelling activities so far!

# Connecting with SCIENCE

## Animals, Birds, and Insects Too!

For each category, list 6 animals that:
- a) fly
- b) are larger than a horse
- c) lay eggs
- d) have feathers
- e) have fur
- f) are smaller than a mouse

## Animal Collectives

Certain animal groups have special names. For example: a **flock** of sheep, a **school** of fish, and a **swarm** of mosquitoes. These special animal groups are called **collectives**.

**1.** Match the animal group to the animals. The clues (in brackets) will help you.

A School of Fish

| | | | | |
|---|---|---|---|---|
| 1 | plague (big grasshoppers) | | a) | lions |
| 2 | gaggle (the males are ganders) | | b) | whales |
| 3 | team (they gallop) | | c) | locusts |
| 4 | gam or pod (very big swimmers) | | d) | wolves |
| 5 | pack (howlers) | | e) | geese |
| 6 | pride (animal "kings") | | f) | horses |

**2.** Find the names of some other animal **collectives**. Ask a librarian to help you.

**3.** Use your spelling strategies to learn words that are difficult.

**4.** Draw a picture of 1 of your animal collectives, and give it a title.

**5.** Write 3 interesting sentences about this special animal group.

**6.** Don't forget to **proofread** the final copy of your work. A partner can help you.

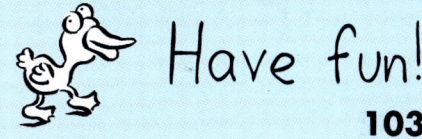

Have fun!

# 27 Suffix -ed

Read this poem about one of the small pleasures of nature.

**The Yellow Tulip**

For weeks it struggled
through the hard crust
of the spring earth
and a foot of air

Just to be
scorched by the sun
jolted by raindrops
blasted by the wind

But on this gentle May morning
as it opens
yellow petals
to the sky

Nothing else matters

— George Swede

## Creating Your Word List

**WORD BOX**

- closed
- skipped
- cried
- tried
- needed
- asked
- missed
- stopped
- picked
- pushed

**Say these words:**

*stepped*   *tried*   *landed*

What sounds does **-ed** make in each word?
The word part **-ed** is a **suffix**. A **suffix** is a group of letters placed at the end of a word. When you add the **suffix -ed** to a **verb**, you make the **past tense**. Like this:

ask + **-ed** = **asked**

Yesterday I **asked** my friend to help me.

1. List words that have the **suffix -ed**. Use the poem "The Yellow Tulip" to help you. Read the words out loud and pay attention to the sound of **-ed** in each word.

2. With your teacher create the list of **-ed** words you will be learning to spell.
You can use: the Word Box, the poem, your own words. These are your Lesson Words

3. **In your notebook**
   - Write the Lesson Words and <u>underline</u> the **suffix -ed**.
   - Keep adding **-ed** words to your Personal Dictionary List. Keep it up to date.

## STRATEGY SPOT

### Snap, Clap, Tap! — Syllables

A **syllable** is a separate sound in a word. Saying a word and quietly snapping, clapping, or tapping out each syllable will help you spell the word correctly.

**QUICK TIP**

When a 1-syllable word ends in a **vowel/consonant pattern**, you double the final consonant before adding **-ed**.
Like this:
ste**p** – ste**pp**ed

# Zoom in on Your Words

1. **Box and Count** Copy your Lesson Words carefully. Draw a box around the **-ed** ending in each word. Quietly snap, clap, or tap out the syllables. How many **syllables** are in each word?

2. **Finish It!** Use words from the Word Box to complete the sentences.
   a) The police officer _____ the traffic at the busy shopping centre.
   b) We _____ strawberries last spring.
   c) I _____ the bus and had to walk.
   d) The store was _____ for holidays.
   e) Stephen _____ to hit the ball with the bat.

3. **Read All About It!** Create 3 newspaper headlines using Lesson Words.
   **TRY THIS!** For an extra challenge, use 2 or more Lesson Words in the SAME headline. For example: **Batter tried but missed ball**

4. **Double Up**  List the words from the Word Box that double the final **consonant** before adding **-ed**. <u>Underline</u> the double consonant. What other words can you add to the list?

5. **Add -ed**  With a partner, SAY the new word that is created when **-ed** is added to each word:
   a) walk     b) climb    c) hop     d) laugh    e) want
   f) bark     g) skip     h) sail    i) wish     j) drop

   **TRY THIS!**  For an extra challenge, SPELL each new word out loud.

6. **What's My Rule?**  Read over each group of words. Match each group of words to the rule it follows when **-ed** is added.
   1  stop/stopped, hum/hummed, step/stepped
   2  pick/picked, wish/wished, rain/rained
   3  cry/cried, dry/dried, copy/copied

   > a)  Change the **y** to **i**.
   > b)  Double the final consonant.
   > c)  Just add **-ed**.

7. **y to i**  Add **-ed** to the following words. For example: bur**y** – bur**ied**. Use each new word in an interesting sentence. Remember to **proofread**.
   a) bury    b) cry    c) copy    d) apply

8. **Exploding Words!**  Watch the word **dry** "explode"!

   dries   dried   dry   drying   undried

   Explode the words below by adding **-s**, **-ed**, **-ing**, **un-**. Write as many new words as you can. Use a dictionary to make sure each new word makes sense.
   a) ask    b) paint    c) close    d) worry

**AT HOME**

9. **An Interesting Word Collage**  Look around your home for interesting words. You might find them in magazines, newspapers, flyers, or food labels. Make a collage of words in your home. See page 37 in Lesson 8 for instructions on how to make a word collage.

## Focus on Language ▶ Dictionary Sections

When you look up words in the dictionary, it helps to think, "Is the word near the beginning, or near the end of the book?" You can imagine your dictionary divided into 2 parts: **a** to **m**, and **n** to **z**. We call **a–m section 1** of the alphabet, and **n–z section 2**.

**1.** Write the Lesson Words you would find in **section 1** (**a–m**).

**2.** Write the Lesson Words you would find in **section 2** (**n–z**).

**3.** Find 3 interesting words in the dictionary. See if your partner can find them quickly in the dictionary using **sections** to help.

**4.** Complete these sentences in 2 ways. First, with a word from **section 1** of the dictionary (**a–m**). Second, with a word from **section 2** (**n–z**).

a) The boy's favourite colour is    1 _____ .
                                                           2 _____ .

b) My best friend is very    1 _____ .
                                                       2 _____ .

c) Lin likes to eat    1 _____ .
                                              2 _____ .

d) I think people should be more    1 _____ .
                                                                                              2 _____ .

### FLASHBACK

Think about the last time you used a dictionary. What made it difficult to find a word? What made it easy?

# 28 Suffixes -less and -able

See how the jigsaw puzzle pieces make new words.

**Remember:** A **suffix** is a group of letters added to the end of a word to make a new word. The **suffix -less** means "without." The **suffix -able** means "capable of" or "worthy of."

## Creating Your Word List

**WORD BOX**

fearless
endless
helpless
careless
useless
comfortable
lovable
valuable
removable
dependable

**Say these words:**
- Say the new word created when the **suffix -less** is added:
  care, help, home, tooth
- Say the new word created when the **suffix -able** is added:
  drink, comfort, remove, depend

1. Make a list of words that use the **suffix -less** and words that use the **suffix -able**. Use the Word Box and jigsaw puzzle to help you.

2. Work with your teacher to create the list of **-less** and **-able** Lesson Words.
   You can use: the Word Box, the puzzle, your own words. These are your Lesson Words.
   As you read each word out loud, STRESS **-less** and **-able**.

3. **In your notebook**
   - Write the Lesson Words and <u>underline</u> the **suffixes -less** and **-able**.
   - You may want to add **-less** and **-able** words to your Personal Dictionary List to help in your reading and writing.

108

# Zoom in on Your Words

1. **Fingerprinting** Look at each of your Lesson Words. Use your finger to "print" each word on your desk. Softly say each word to yourself. Listen to all the sounds.

2. **Syllable Count** The word **com • fort • a • ble** has 4 **syllables**. Count the number of syllables in each of your Lesson Words.

3. **–less Words** **Fearless** means "without fear." Write the meanings of these words:
   a) careless    b) endless    c) useless
   d) painless    e) helpless   f) speechless

4. **Word Machine** The new-word machine adds the **suffix** **-able** to words that go in it. Put these words through the new-word machine:
   a) love    b) remove    c) value
   d) use     e) manage    f) replace

**TRY THIS!** What is the rule for adding **-able** to words that end in **e**? Write this rule in your own words.

## STRATEGY SPOT

### Remember! — Mnemonic Devices

A little saying can help you remember the spelling of a tricky word. For example:

Have a **ball** with a **ball**oon.
You h**ear** with an **ear**.

I'd like to have **2** de**ss**erts.
The princi**pal** is your **pal**.

A saying, poem, or picture that helps you remember the spelling of a word is called a **mnemonic device**. Look up **mnemonic** in your dictionary.

**5. Match Up!** Match each word with its meaning:

1  reliable         a) providing comfort
2  comfortable      b) can be relied on
3  removable        c) worthy of love
4  lovable          d) having worth
5  valuable         e) can be removed

**TRY THIS!** For an extra challenge, make clues for 3 of your Lesson Words. Share them with a partner.

**6. Root It Out!** Write the **root word** for each of the following:

a) careless     b) helpless     c) lovable
d) dependable   e) reliable     f) valuable

AT HOME

**7. Elemenno/LMNO** Play at home! Pick a Lesson Word. Start with the FIRST letter of your word, then write the next 4 letters in the alphabet. Use words that start with those 5 letters to make a silly sentence. Like this:

**C**omfortable **d**ucks **e**at **f**resh **g**rass.

**TRY THIS!** For an extra challenge, ask someone at home to help you write 2 more Elemennos.

**8. Quite a Challenge** Select the correct **challenge word** from the pair to complete each sentence.

a) Prairie dogs are (**desert/dessert**) mammals.
b) Dad always reminds me to (**clothes/close**) the door.
c) In math, we will study (**angels/angles**).
d) That was (**quite/quiet**) the storm we had last night.

Add each word pair to your list of challenge words.

QUICK TIP

**9. Exploding Words** Watch the word **suit** "explode"!

Explode these words. Use a dictionary to check your new words.

a) use     b) help     c) love     d) know

When the **suffix -able** is added to some words, the final silent **e** is dropped. For example: lov**e** – **lovable**

## Focus on Language ▶ Confusables

**Homophones** (words that sound alike but have different spellings and meanings) are often confused. For example: **its** and **it's**.
**Its** shows ownership:

> The cat played with **its** toy mouse.
> Put the box down on **its** side.

**It's** is the **contraction** for **it is**:

> I think **it's** time for recess.
> **It's** my coat that is dirty.

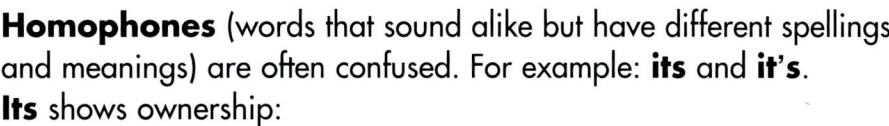

**1.** Write **its** or **it's** to complete the sentences.
   a) The cat licked _____ paws.
   b) When Mr. Yuen arrives, _____ time to go home.

**Their**, **there**, and **they're** are also confusing.
**Their** shows ownership:

> **Their** dog ran away.
> What is **their** last name?

**There** refers to a place:

> Put the cake over **there** near the dishes.
> Don't stand here. Go over **there**.

**They're** is the contraction for **they are**:

> **They're** going to the beach for a picnic.
> Did you know **they're** the fastest runners on the team?

**2.** Choose **there**, **their**, or **they're** to complete these sentences.
   a) _____ dog's name is Casey.
   b) My teacher said _____ going to join us over _____ .

### FLASHBACK

Can you think of a **saying** to help you remember how to choose the correct spelling of these confusable words?

# 29 -y, -ay

Here are some silly knock-knock jokes to read and enjoy.

Knock, knock.
— Who's there?
Ready.
— Ready who?
Ready or not, here I come!

Knock, knock.
— Who's there?
Boo.
— Boo who?
Oh, don't cry!

Knock, knock.
— Who's there?
Lucky.
— Lucky who?
Lucky you, I'm here to stay!

## Creating Your Word List

**WORD BOX**

dirty
mighty
sly
pray
donkey
delay
angry
January
birthday
twenty

**Say these words:**

donkey   cry   birthday

Listen to the sound made by **-y**. What sounds can **-y** make?

1. Make a list of words that end in **-y**. Use the knock-knock jokes to help you. Put the words into a chart like this:

| -y like long e | -y like long i | -ay like long a |
|---|---|---|
|  |  |  |

2. Work with your teacher to create the list of **-y** and **-ay** words you will be spelling.
You can use: the Word Box, the knock-knock jokes, your own words.
Add your Lesson Words to the chart above.

3. **In your notebook**
   - Write the Lesson Words. Circle the **-y** or **-ay** ending in each word.
   - Add new **-y** and **-ay** words that you find to your Personal Dictionary List.

   **TRY THIS!** Make up your own knock-knock jokes using words that end in **-y/-ay**. Share them with a partner.

## STRATEGY SPOT

### Find a Word in a Word

To remember the spelling of words, find the smaller words in them. For example, the word **end** is in **friend**. You can also make up little sayings to help you remember the words in words. For example: A **lawyer** knows the **law**. Find smaller words in your Lesson Words to help you remember the spelling.

# Zoom in on Your Words

1. **Word Darts** Ready to play darts? Match these numbers to the words.

## QUICK TIP

In a word that ends in **-y**, the **y** is a **vowel** and makes a **long vowel sound**: **a**, **e**, or **i**.

2. **Missing Vowels** The computer is acting silly again! It skipped some letters. Fill in the missing **vowels** to make words. All the words end in **-y**.

   a) d _ rt _   b) _ ngr _   c) d _ l _ _
   d) J _ n _ _ r _   e) d _ nk _ _   f) m _ ght _
   g) sl _   h) t _ en _ _

   **TRY THIS!** For an extra challenge, make up 4 of your own missing-vowel puzzles.

113

**3. Rhyme Time** Write words that rhyme with each of the following:
   a) sunny    b) day    c) cry

**4. A Wordy Pole** Use the clues to write Lesson Words. The word in the pole will tell how you feel on your birthday.

a) an icy sport
b) opposite of **difficult**
c) a young dog
d) a small coin
e) this opens doors

a) _ _ _ _ _ y
b) _ _ _ y
c) _ _ _ _ y
d) _ _ _ _ y
e) _ _ y

## AT HOME

**5. Stormy Weather** Listen to the weather report. Make a list of weather words that end in **-y**.
   **TRY THIS!** For an extra challenge, illustrate a weather word ending in **-y**, using letters that look like rain, snow, sunny skies, and so on.

**6. What Happened Here?** Watch what happens when we make these **-y** words **plural** (mean more than one).

   la**dy** – la**dies**, ba**by** – ba**bies**, ru**by** – ru**bies**

Make these words mean more than one:
   a) country    b) cherry    c) family
   d) penny      e) puppy     f) bunny

**TRY THIS!** For an extra challenge, write the rule that tells what happened to the **y** in these plurals.

## QUICK TIP

**7. More Plurals** Make these words **plural**:
   a) day       b) monkey    c) delay
   d) turkey    e) donkey    f) tray

Did you remember to just add **-s** to each word?

To form the **plural** of words ending in **-ay**, **-ey**, or **-oy**, just add **-s**.

### DID YOU KNOW?

The word **ox** is the only animal name that forms its **plural** by adding **-en**: ox – ox**en**.

114

## Focus on Language ▶ Irregular Plurals

Most words form the **plural** by adding **-s** or **-es**. But some words do not follow that rule. Some words that end in **-f** or **-fe** form the plural by changing the **f** to a **v** and adding **-es**:

ca**lf** – ca**lves**
loa**f** – loa**ves**

**1.** Make these words **plural** by changing **f** to **v** and adding **-es**.

    **a)** elf      **b)** leaf      **c)** half
    **d)** wolf      **e)** life      **f)** knife

**TRY THIS!** For an extra challenge, use 3 of the plurals in interesting sentences. Don't forget to **proofread**.

**2.** Make these words plural by just adding **-s**.

    **a)** roof      **b)** cliff      **c)** chief

**3.** Some words form the plural by changing the original word into a different word. For example:

**person – people**

Write the plural of:

    **a)** woman      **b)** man      **c)** child

**4.** Some words form the plural by not changing the original word in ANY way. Words that follow this pattern include **sheep** and **deer**.

**TRY THIS!** For an extra challenge, make a list of all the ways to form plurals. Put this list in your Personal Dictionary or writing folder.

### FLASHBACK

You have learned several things about words that end in the letter **y**. Tell 2 things that you learned in this lesson.

# 30 SPELL CHECK

## REVIEW

**Patterns**

ir, or, ur
pr- and ex-
suffix -ed
suffixes -less and -able
-y, -ay

**Strategies**

1. Pronounce words clearly!
2. Build word families by sound.
3. Clap, snap, tap! — Syllables.
4. Remember! — Mnemonic devices.
5. Find a word in a word.

## Creating Your Word List

**In your notebook**
- Go to your list of "Words I Still Need to Practise."
- Pick 10 words you need to practise spelling.

## Zoom in on Your Words

1. **Be a Slowpoke**  S...l...o...w...l...y say each word to yourself. **Pronounce** each sound clearly.

2. **Underline It**  Use a coloured pencil to underline the part of the word you need to focus on.

3. **Snap, Clap, Tap!**  Pick 4 Lesson Words and snap, clap, or tap out the **syllables** in each word.

4. **A Wordy Province**  How many different words can you make using the letters in the name **Prince Edward Island**? Try to come up with more than your partner does.

5. **Word Formulas**  Complete these formulas to write the new words.
   a) love – e + able =
   b) end + less + ly =
   c) birth + day =
   d) copy – y + i + ed =

   **TRY THIS!**  For an extra challenge, make up 3 of your own word formulas to share with a partner.

6. **Alphasort**  Sort these words into alphabetical order.
   a) produce
   b) prize
   c) proper
   d) Prince Edward Island
   e) present
   f) promise

AT HOME

7. **Study Your Spelling Words** Look at the Strategy Spot on page 25 in Lesson 5. Use some of the 6 study skills to practise your Lesson Words.

8. **Twenty-Word Search** Find 20 words you have studied in the past 5 lessons and write them in your notebook.

| u | g | o | s | k | i | p | p | e | d | r | g | g | d |
|---|---|---|---|---|---|---|---|---|---|---|---|---|---|
| d | c | p | r | o | d | u | c | e | s | t | s | m | l |
| s | z | n | f | n | s | u | a | m | q | r | r | o | r |
| t | s | e | h | h | f | c | l | p | u | o | f | f | o |
| i | s | e | e | k | k | i | d | g | i | t | j | l | w |
| q | j | d | l | e | p | o | x | a | r | o | s | u | e |
| t | t | e | r | p | n | y | u | u | r | m | s | x | t |
| p | u | d | r | k | l | t | u | y | e | e | a | l | p |
| r | s | r | e | q | h | e | t | m | l | m | o | x | e |
| o | d | y | t | o | s | n | h | e | p | v | k | s | c |
| m | o | r | r | l | e | e | s | l | a | i | g | f | x |
| i | w | z | i | w | e | s | e | b | y | v | g | u | e |
| s | g | r | t | h | o | l | l | o | y | t | r | i | d |
| e | g | v | m | u | t | e | y | t | h | g | i | m | x |

9. **Sort Out Your Words!** Write each of your Lesson Words on small pieces of paper. Think of different ways to sort your words: Sort by meaning, sort by spelling pattern, sort by **consonant sound**, sort by **vowel sound**.

10. **Memory Helpers** Pick a Lesson Word that is giving you problems. Think of a saying (**mnemonic device**) that will help you remember how to spell it. See the Strategy Spot on page 109 in Lesson 28 for help. Share your **mnemonic device** with a partner.

## FLASHBACK

Look at the Lesson Words that you now know how to spell. Cross them off your list of "Words I Still Need to Practise." Excellent work! You are now a spelling superstar!

# 31 Silent Letter Review

It's time to review what we have learned about silent letters. Can you find all the silent letters in this spooky poem?

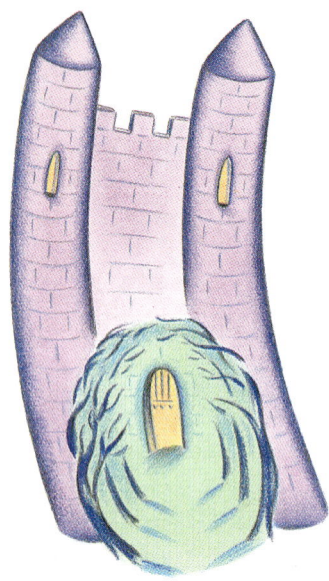

Dare you enter
   into the castle
      of the ghost?
Climb the stairs,
   explore the dungeons
      of this frightening place.
Listen, listen!
What's that sound?
   Knocking knees,
      sweating palms —
         numb with fear.
Will you make it
   through the visit?

## Creating Your Word List

**WORD BOX**

knee
knife
half
write
talk
castle
listen
caught
climb
numb
wrist
lamb

**Say these words:**

ghost   wrap   comb   walk

All of these words have **silent letters**. Which letters are seen but not heard?

1. As a class, make a list of words that have **silent letters**. Use the poem to help you. Put the words into a chart like this:

| silent letter at beginning | silent letter at end | silent letter inside word |
|---|---|---|
|  |  |  |

118

2. Work with your teacher to create the list of **silent letter** words you will be learning to spell.
You can use: the Word Box, the poem, your own words. These are your Lesson Words.

3. **In your notebook**
   - Write the Lesson Words. Circle the **silent letters**.
   - Can you find some words in your Personal Dictionary List that have **silent letters**?

QUICK TIP

**A** or **an**? Be sure to use **an** before a word that begins with a **vowel** or a silent letter **h**. For example: **a** holiday, **an** igloo, **an** honest person

# Zoom in on Your Words

1. **Wordprint Match-Up** Copy the wordprints and match each word with its wordprint shape in your notebook.

   wrist, castle, caught, listen, wren, honest, numb, knife

   a)   b)   c)   d)
   e)   f)   g)   h)

2. **Word Sort** Sort the words from the Word Box into this chart.

   | silent **k** | silent **w** | silent **b** | silent **t** | silent **gh** |
   |---|---|---|---|---|
   | | | | | |

3. **Crack the Code!** Copy each sentence and complete each word that is missing **silent letters**.
   a) We will meet at one _ our after midni _ _ t.
   b) I will w _ is _ le to let you _ now where I am.
   c) Lis _ en carefully! You mi _ _ t be ha _ f asleep.
   d) Be sure to wear your wa _ ch on your _ rist.

4. **Is That a or an?** Use each of these words in a short sentence. Put **a** or **an** before each word:
   a) hour     b) ghost     c) knife
   d) honour   e) heart     f) half

119

5. **Wake the Sleeping k!** In words that begin with the **kn-** pattern, the **k** is usually silent. Wake the sleeping **k** and copy and solve these riddles. The clues will help you.

a) part of the leg
b) sounds the same as **night**
c) a loud tap at the door
d) it cuts things
e) sounds the same as **no**

a) _ _ _ _
b) _ _ _ _ _ _
c) _ _ _ _ _
d) _ _ _ _ _
e) _ _ _ _

**TRY THIS!** For an extra challenge, make clues for 3 of your Lesson Words. Share them with a partner.

6. **Silly Silent Sentences** With a partner, write 3 silly sentences using as many words with **silent letters** as you can. For example:

   We **k**nit soc**k**s for **h**onourable **k**nig**h**ts.

## STRATEGY SPOT

### Words Alive! — Use the Thesaurus

A **thesaurus** is a kind of dictionary that gives us words that mean the same as and opposite to the word we look up. Words in the thesaurus are arranged in alphabetical order. Look in the thesaurus to give yourself a choice of interesting words.

**AT HOME**

7. **Silent Letter Search** Make a list of names of family, friends, and neighbours. Put an **X** through the **silent letters** in these names.

## FLASHBACK

What are some things you've learned about **silent letters**?

# Connecting with Literature

### The Velveteen Rabbit

There was once a velveteen rabbit, and in the beginning he was really splendid. He was fat and bunchy, as a rabbit should be; his coat was spotted brown and white, he had real thread whiskers, and his ears were lined with pink sateen. On Christmas morning, when he sat wedged in the top of the Boy's stocking, with a sprig of holly between his paws, the effect was charming.

— from *The Velveteen Rabbit* by Margery Williams

**1.** In the opening paragraph of her book, the author has used interesting words and phrases to describe the toy stuffed rabbit. Find the describing words and phrases that give us a clear picture of the rabbit in our minds.

**2.** Draw a picture of what the velveteen rabbit might look like.

**3.** Look up the word **splendid** in a thesaurus. Write the words that mean the same as **splendid**.

**4.** Select 1 of your own stories. Read it over, searching for overused and boring words. Use a **thesaurus** to help you add variety to your word use.

Imagine the wonderful, impressive, amazing, and exciting stories you can write with the help of the thesaurus!

# 32 Homophone Review

Let's review what we have learned about **homophones**. Remember, homophones are words that sound the same but have different spellings and meanings. There are lots of homophones in this chant!

"Flee!" said my father
to the flea on his dog.
"Shoo!" said my aunt
to the fly on her shoe.
"Heal!" said my cousin
to the sore on her heel.
"Gym!" said my brother
to his best friend, Jim.

## Creating Your Word List

**WORD BOX**

threw
through
dear
deer
peace
piece
aunt
ant
tale
tail
past
passed
its
it's

**Say these pairs of words:**

see/sea   pear/pair   so/sew   close/clothes

What is the meaning of each word? What other pairs of **homophones** do you know?

1. Make a list of pairs of words that are **homophones**. Use the chant to help you.

2. Work with your teacher to create the list of **homophone pairs** you will be learning to spell.
   You can use: the Word Box, the chant, your own words. These are your Lesson Words.
   **TRY THIS!** For an extra challenge, can you think of a **homophone trio** — 3 words that sound the same but have different spellings and meanings?

## STRATEGY SPOT

### Proofreading — Does It Look Right?

When proofreading your work, circle any words that do not look right. Now check your circled words in a dictionary, in your Personal Dictionary List, or ask someone else. When writing, get your ideas down FIRST and then go back and double-check any spellings you are not sure of.

**QUICK TIP**

Knowing which **homophone** to use can be tricky. Make sure that you listen very carefully to the sentence so that you'll know which word to use.

# Zoom in on Your Words

1. **Copy and Shape It!** Copy your Lesson Words carefully. Draw the **wordprint** shape for each word.

2. **Pick a Homophone** Choose the correct **homophone** to complete each sentence:
   a) We saw a (**dear/deer**) in the forest.
   b) I sent my (**aunt/ant**) a thank-you card.
   c) The children sang a song about (**peace/piece**) on Earth.
   d) The happy puppy was wagging (**its/it's**) tail.

3. **Pair Up** Use each of the following **homophone pairs** in a sentence. Like this:

   where/wear — My friend said, "**Where** will you ever **wear** that?"

4. **Pass on By** The words **past** and **passed** often confuse us. **Past** is a **noun** that means "time gone by." The **verb passed** means "went or moved by." Choose **past** or **passed** to complete each sentence:
   a) The time is now fifteen _____ eleven.
   b) We _____ Ahmed's house on the way here.
   c) Forget about it, that's all in the _____ .

5. **Not That One!** Christina needs help understanding this letter. Replace each underlined word with the correct **homophone**.

Deer Christina,
Eye wood like to tell ewe about my holiday. Eye road on a hoarse, picked pairs, and sat in the son on the beech. Next time, maybe ewe wood like to join us. My ant wood knot mind if you came to visit for a few daze.
                      Your friend,
                      Sonia

6. **Homophone Crossword** Choose the correct word from the **homophone pairs** and write them in your notebook.

creak/creek, brake/break, read/red,
pair/pear, sail/sale, cent/sent

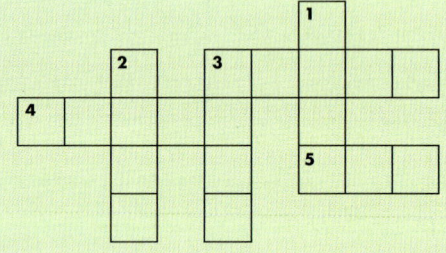

**Across**
3 a small stream
4 this stops a car
5 a colour that says "stop"

**Down**
1 a fruit
2 part of a boat the wind blows
3 a penny

AT HOME

7. **And the Message Is ...**
On the way home, look at car licence plates. Sometimes they have a message or saying. Someone in a hurry may have the licence plate **NVRL8**. An eye doctor might have a plate that says **I C U**. Invent a personal licence plate of your own. Remember to write no more than 6 letters and/or numbers.

# FLASHBACK

How would you describe yourself as a speller? What 2 spelling strategies do you use when you write?

# Connecting with Social Studies

## What's in a Name?

**How did cities, towns, and villages get their names?**

The origin of the names of cities can be fascinating. There are many reasons why towns have the names they have. Some towns and cities were named after the first European settler. Other towns and cities were given the names of places (**London**, Ontario) and people (**Victoria**, British Columbia) in Europe, because the early settlers were homesick. A few names were clerical errors. Some towns and cities first had Aboriginal names. For example, **Kingston** was originally called **Catarqui**, an Aboriginal word for "rocks standing in water." Some places, such as **Squamish** and **Ottawa**, have kept a form of an Aboriginal name.

How do you think these towns got their names?

1. Do some research to find out how your town or city got its name. There are books in the library to help you get this information.

2. What is the name of your school? How do you think it got its name?

3. What are the names of the streets around your school? How do you think they got their names?

4. Draw a silhouette of your town on a sheet of paper and add the information you found in questions **1** to **3**.

Next time you go on a car trip, take note of the names of the towns you pass and try to figure out how they got their names.

# Spelling STRETCH

**SPELLING STRETCH**

Find out more about words and make your spelling skills stretch in this special section of exciting games and extra challenges. Your teacher will show you which activities are just for YOU.

1. **Sign Up!** The word **sign** is a **root word**. Read these words which have **sign** as the root:

   **assign, signpost, design, resign,
   signal, signature, significant**

   What happened to the **i sound**? In some words the **long i** changed to a **short i sound**. The root is still spelled the same way, but the sound changes. Fill in the chart with the **sign** words and underline the word **sign** in each word.

   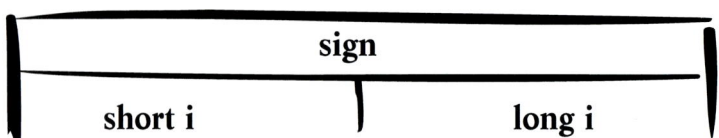

2. **Little Ones** List the smaller words in each of these words. Do not change the order of the letters.
   - a) tired
   - b) flight
   - c) stride
   - d) spine
   - e) bright
   - f) grind
   - g) price
   - h) bicycle
   - i) thigh
   - j) alike
   - k) outside

3. **Hink-Pink**
   a) A riddle with a rhyming pair of words as the answer is a **hink-pink**. For example: What do you call a soaking dog or cat? A **wet pet**. Write a riddle for each of the following hink-pinks.
   1. fun run
   2. rude dude
   3. damp camp
   4. fright night

   b) Think up some of your own **hink-pinks** to share with the class.

4. **Opposites Attract** Write the opposite (**antonym**) for each of these words:
   - a) cruel
   - b) wrong
   - c) inside
   - d) day
   - e) tame
   - f) loose
   - g) awake
   - h) frown

**SPELLING STRETCH**

**5. Food Crossword** Many of our words for food have come from other languages. Use the clues to solve this food-word puzzle. Copy the words into your notebook.

**Across**
4. This umbrella-shaped fungus gets its name from a Middle French word, **mousseron**.
5. **Askútasquash** is the Algonkian word for this vegetable.
7. **Koekje** is the Dutch word for this little, crisp cake.
8. The Greek word **daktylos** named this fruit.
11. The Persian word **narang** named this juicy fruit.
13. The Latin word **union** named this teary vegetable.
14. The Middle English word **mete** rhymes with our word.
15. The Italian word **brocco** named this vegetable.

**Down**
1. The Greek word **pepon**, meaning "ripened in the sun," named this Hallowe'en ornament.
2. From an Old English word, **breowan**, meaning "to brew"; used to make toast.
3. From the Latin word **radix**, meaning "root."
6. From the Latin word **vegetabilis**, meaning "growing."
7. From the Old French word **caboche**, meaning "head"; looks like lettuce.
9. The Italian word **cavolfiore**, meaning "cabbage flower," named this vegetable.
10. The Old English word **korn** named this grain.
12. From the Spanish word **batata**; made into chips.

6. **Word Mobile**  Make a list of words on a theme. For example, words about the **weather**, **sports**, or **foods**. Cut out shapes of construction paper; use different-coloured paper. Hang them from a hanger to make a **mobile**.

7. **Challenging Problems**  Solve each of these **challenge word** problems:

   a) Ms. Angel ordered a new sign for the hardware store. Should she pay for the sign? Why not?

   > Ms. Angle's Hardwaer Store
   > … In bussines since 1980

   b) Anna wanted some take-out food for lunch. What's wrong with the menu?

   | Cheseburger | $2.50 |
   | French fryes | $1.50 |
   | Hot dogg | $2.00 |
   | Milk shache | $1.75 |
   | Aple Pie | $1.50 |

   c) Cheung received an invitation to Kelly's birthday party. Spot the spelling mistakes.

   > Come to a Birthday Partey
   > When: Saterday, Novumber 19
   > Time: at one o'clok
   > Where: 16 Main Streat
   > For: Kelly's Birthday Partee

8. **Add-a-Letter**  Add a letter to each word to make a new word. For example, add a letter to **super** to make a meal: **supper**. Add a letter to
   a) **pant** to make something colourful
   b) **cod** to make you shiver
   c) **nap** to make a sound
   d) **raw** to make a picture
   e) **word** to make our earth
   f) **plant** to make something in outer space
   g) **bed** to make something you find on a necklace

SPELLING STRETCH

**9. Change-a-Letter**

a) Do this activity with a partner. Choose a word. Change one letter to create a new word. Change another letter and make another new word. For example:

send – **l**end – le**a**d – **r**ead – ...

b) See how many new words you can make with each of these words:

1 date    2 best    3 line

**10. The Same But Different**

a) Use **homophone pairs** to solve each clue. For example:

two of a kind/a fruit – **pair/pear**

1 a colourful plant part/a baking ingredient
2 a dog wags this/a fable
3 comes after seven/a past tense of **eat**
4 a penny/a smell
5 to take without permission/a metal

b) Use a pair of homophones to complete each sentence:

1 Out of the dozen cookies, Max _____ four and now there are _____ left.
2 Which _____ does the needle point when you get on the scale to _____ yourself?
3 It was a beautiful day with a pretty _____ sky, and the wind _____ softly through the trees.
4 I _____ _____ -handed, but my sister writes left-handed.
5 After we had _____ the last game, we had only _____ more game before the championships.

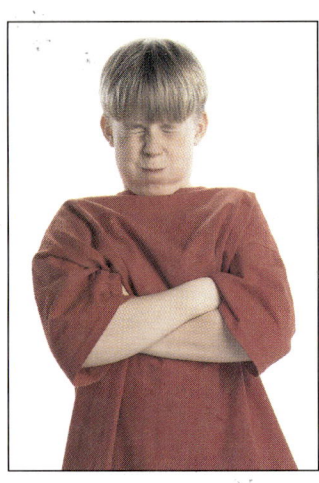

## 11. Idioms

a) Match each idiom with its meaning.

| Idiom | Meaning |
|---|---|
| down in the dumps | nervous, scared |
| butterflies in your stomach | wait for a long time |
| under the weather | depressed, sad |
| all thumbs | in trouble |
| pigheaded | clumsy, awkward |
| hold your breath | ill, sick |
| simmer down | stubborn |
| up a tree | angry, furious |
| hit the ceiling | relax, calm yourself |

b) Choose 2 of the idioms in **a)**. For each one, write a sentence or two about a time when YOU felt like that.

c) Read the following idioms. Pick 3 and draw a picture that describes what the words say but NOT what they mean.
1. pull the wool over your eyes
2. a wolf in sheep's clothing
3. sound asleep
4. put your foot in your mouth
5. cry crocodile tears
6. rack one's brains

## 12. What Is That?

a) What do you think the word **ukulele** means? Draw a picture of it, and then check in the dictionary to see if your meaning matches the real meaning.

b) Do this game with a partner. Look in the dictionary for a word. Have your partner draw a picture of what it means. Then show him or her the dictionary meaning.

## 13. Kennings

a) **Toe-warmers** and **foot-holders** tell what socks and shoes DO, but are funny ways of saying **socks** and **shoes**. Describing an ordinary thing this way instead of using a simple name is called a **kenning**.

SPELLING STRETCH

Here are some other kennings:
A **hat** could be a **head-house**.
A **coat** could be a **body-protector**.

Make up kennings for each of these items:
1  jeans      2  scarf      3  boots
4  umbrella   5  button     6  pocket

b) Choose 3 of your kennings and use each in a sentence. Pass your sentences to your partner to see if he or she can figure out what items you are describing.

## 14. Invent a Thing, Invent a Word!

a) Draw a picture of something that you would like to invent. Give your invention a name. It does not need to be a real word.

b) Make up a word. Draw the meaning of that word. Show your inventions to a partner.

## 15. Where Is That Place?

a) Many towns and cities in Canada have interesting names. Find these towns on a map of Canada. What province/territory are they in? How do you think each of these places got its name?

1  Yellowknife        2  Moose Jaw
3  Smooth Rock Falls  4  Corner Brook
5  Medicine Hat       6  Trois-Rivières

b) Can you find other interesting place names? Make up a story to tell how 1 of these places got its name.

## 16. Proverbs
Read each **proverb**. Then change the ending to make a new one. Have fun!

a) the early bird (gets the worm)
b) haste makes (waste)
c) a stitch in time (saves nine)
d) hard work (never killed anyone)
e) laugh and the world laughs with you (cry and you cry alone)
f) don't cry over (spilled milk)
g) early to bed (early to rise)
h) when the cat's away (the mouse will play)

**17. What Language Is This?** Here is the word **friend** in many different languages:

| "Friend" | | Language |
|---|---|---|
| 1 | yoojeen _____ | Japanese |
| | nemukw _____ | Qwakw'ala |
| | cairde _____ | Irish |
| | cariad _____ | Welsh |
| | ne cho o ga n _____ | Cree |
| | droog _____ | Russian |

| 2 | ami | German |
|---|---|---|
| | amigo | Hungarian |
| | amico | Latin |
| | amicus | Italian |
| | barát | Spanish |
| | freund | French |

| 3 | chaver | Portuguese |
|---|---|---|
| | péng-you | Korean |
| | amigo | Arabic |
| | chingoo | Hebrew |
| | hbib | Polish |
| | przyjaciel | Chinese |

a) In your notebook, match the words with the languages they come from. The first box is done for you. (Qwakw'ala and Cree are North American Aboriginal languages.)

b) What do you notice about some of the words? Write a little story to one of your friends and tell why you like being friends with that person. **Proofread** your story carefully.

c) Print the word **friend** in many languages to make a border.

d) Roll up your story in a scroll and give it to your friend.

**SPELLING STRETCH**

**18. I'm Thinking of a Word** Play this game with a partner. Player A thinks of a word and gives Player B one clue at a time. For example:

1) I'm thinking of a **ch** word.
2) It has 6 letters.
3) It ends in a **y**.
4) It grows on a tree.
5) It is a red fruit.

Answer: **cherry**

Now take turns playing the game with a partner. Choose your own words.

**19. High Fives!**

a) Trace your hand and cut it out carefully. On each finger and on the thumb tell:
   1 your goals as a speller
   2 what you have learned in spelling
   3 a **challenge word** you can now spell
   4 a fun spelling activity
   5 your favourite Personal Dictionary word to say

b) Make a list of 5 good things about:
   1 learning to spell
   2 your class
   3 your teacher
   4 your family
   5 your friends

c) Use this information to fill in a chart.

**20. Spelling Banners** Make a banner. On the banner write a joke or a tongue twister or a riddle. Share your banner with a partner.

**21. Canadian Word Puzzle** Use the clues to help you choose the **Canadian Words** that solve this puzzle. Write the words in your notebook.

**Canadian Words**
muskrat
parka
grubstake
coureur de bois
bannock
gopher
tundra
toboggan
cheechako
sourdough

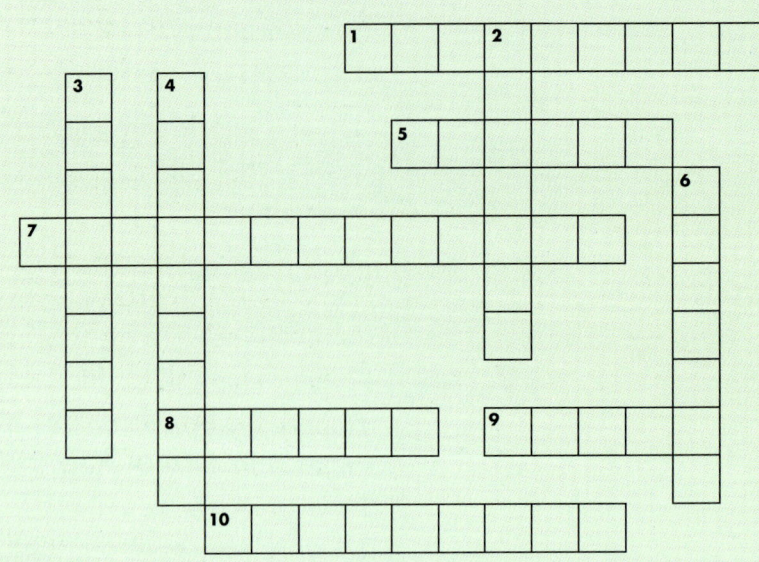

### Across

1. This Klondike gold-rush word described a loan of food and equipment in return for a share of any gold found.
5. This Russian word names a large, treeless place in the Arctic.
7. This French Canadian name for a fur trader means "runner of the woods."
8. This name for an animal that lives underground came from the French Canadian word **gaufre**.
9. This Inuit word meaning "outer skin" names a winter coat.
10. This Yukon word, meaning "newcomer," came from the Chinook people.

### Down

2. This Scottish Gaelic word names a type of thin oatmeal cake.
3. The Micmac word meaning "handsled" named this long, flat sleigh.
4. This Klondike word names a kind of bread that was important in the Yukon.
6. The Algonkian people named this water rodent.

SPELLING STRETCH

**22. Sports Words and Pictures** If someone wrote a dictionary just for hockey players, words like **skates**, **puck**, **score**, **stick**, and **face-off** would be in it.

a) Choose a sport from the list below. Make a player's dictionary. Write 10 words that would go in your dictionary. Put the words in alphabetical order.

| tennis | soccer | baseball | gymnastics |
| figure skating | lacrosse | badminton | football |
| basketball | hockey | | |

b) Make a small card (15 cm x 10 cm). Draw your favourite athlete on the front. On the back talk about that athlete. Make a few cards for your class. As a class, put them into a box to make your own class collection of favourite athletes.

**23. Fingerspelling** People sometimes use their fingers to spell words:

a) Spell out your name using fingerspelling.
b) Spell out 5 **challenge words**.
c) Spell out a partner's name.
d) See if you can carry on a simple conversation with a partner, using fingerspelling.

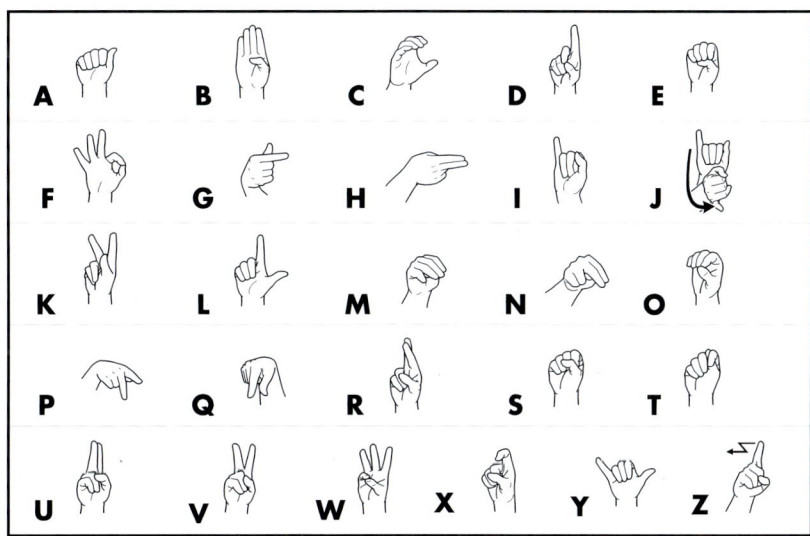

**24. Calligraphy** The word **calligraphy** means "beautiful writing." You can use a special pen to write in calligraphy. Look at these words written in calligraphy.

*question    favourite*

  a) What do you notice about the script?
  b) Write 5 words from your Personal Dictionary List in fancy calligraphy script.

**25. Speed Spelling** On a piece of paper, write down the letters of the alphabet in any order. Write the letters more than once. Now look over your page. Spell words by circling letters. **Consonants** can only be used once, but **vowels** can be used as often as you like.

**26. Clichés** A **cliché** is a common phrase that describes something. The actual words do not have to make sense but the phrase is understood. For example, "**fight like cats and dogs**" means that they were really fighting. Clichés are often overused.

  a) Match the first and second half of each cliché phrase. Write the complete cliché in your notebook.

| | | | |
|---|---|---|---|
| 1 | cried like … | a) | hotcakes |
| 2 | eats like … | b) | a chimney |
| 3 | came out smelling like … | c) | a lead balloon |
| 4 | I know this place like … | d) | a horse |
| 5 | melts like … | e) | roses |
| 6 | runs like … | f) | a baby |
| 7 | sank like … | g) | honey |
| 8 | selling like … | h) | the back of my hand |
| 9 | slept like … | i) | the wind |
| 10 | smokes like … | j) | a baby |

  b) Use the name of a piece of clothing to complete each phrase:
   1 to have something up your …
   2 hot under the …
   3 cute as a …

**SPELLING STRETCH**

4   a stuffed ...
5   a wolf in sheep's ...
6   a feather in one's ...

c) Choose 4 of the cliché phrases in **a)** and **b)**. Draw a picture that describes what the words say but NOT what they mean.

d) Pick 3 other clichés and rewrite each one using your own words.

## 27. A Gathering of Animals

a) Match the columns to complete phrases that name **animal collectives**:

| | | | |
|---|---|---|---|
| 1 | a warren of ... | a) | clams |
| 2 | a colony of ... | b) | rabbits |
| 3 | a bed of ... | c) | bees |
| 4 | a crash of ... | d) | ants |
| 5 | a swarm of ... | e) | rhinoceroses |
| 6 | a school of ... | f) | monkeys |
| 7 | a troop of ... | g) | fish |
| 8 | a clutch of ... | h) | elephants |
| 9 | a flock of ... | i) | chickens |
| 10 | a herd of ... | j) | sheep |

b) Illustrate 1 of these groups. For example, show **fish** at **school**. Title your picture in your notebook.

## 28. Design It!

a) What kind of running shoes do you wear? What is the **logo** for the company? Design a logo for a pair of shoes.

b) Look at some different stamps. What are the pictures on them? Why were these pictures chosen? Design a stamp with a picture of a famous Canadian on it.

c) Look carefully at some coins: pennies, nickels, dimes, quarters, loonies, toonies. What pictures and words are on them? Design a 3-dollar coin. Cut it out. Make a list of things you would buy with this coin.

## 29. That's Interesting!

a) Look through a library book, a newspaper, or a magazine to find some interesting words.

b) Is the word a **noun** — does it **name** a feeling, an idea, a place, a person? Is it a **verb** — an **action** word? Is it an **adjective** or **adverb** — **describing** words?

c) Find 10 words that you think are interesting. Write the words in fancy printing, using markers and coloured pencils. Show whether each word is a **noun**, **verb**, **adjective**, or **adverb**.

d) Use 3 of your words in interesting sentences.

## 30. Diamond Poems

a) Here is how you write a diamond poem:

1 ........................... land
2 ....................... rocky, flat
3 ................. fields, cities, hills
4 ........... green, soft — blue, deep
5 ............... wave, cool, drops
6 ................... floating, clear
7 ........................... water

Pick 2 things that are opposites.

1 Write 1 of the 2 things on the first line of the poem.
2 On the next line, write 2 words that tell about the thing.
3 Write 3 words that tell about the thing on the next line.
4 On the next line, write 2 more words that remind you of the thing. Then write 2 words that remind you of its OPPOSITE.
5 The next line has 3 words that tell about this opposite thing.
6 The next line has only 2 words that describe the opposite.
7 Finish the poem by writing the opposite.

b) Write your own diamond poem. Choose 1 of these pairs of opposites or use your own ideas.

    sun/shade    smooth/rocky    night/day

**SPELLING STRETCH**

**31. Idea Webs**

a) What do you like best about holidays? Are there some things you DON'T like about holidays? An **Idea Web** can help you organize your thoughts. Can you think of other ideas to add to the 2 webs? Add at least 2 more ideas to each web.

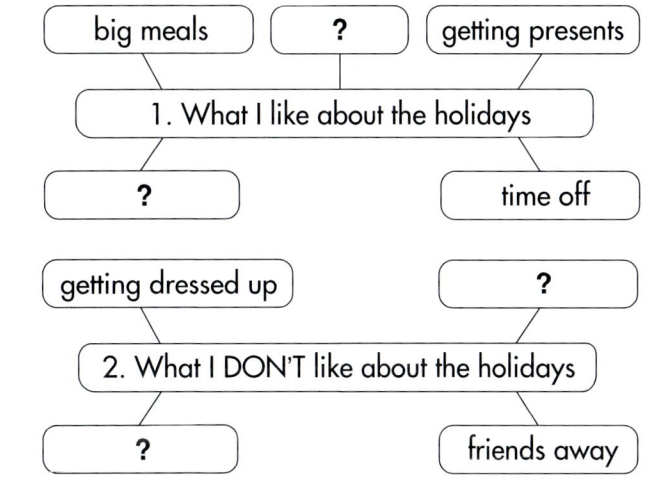

b) Choose a specific holiday and do 2 Idea Webs like the ones above.

c) Create a NEW holiday! Give it a name and pick a time of year to celebrate it. What special things would you do? How long would it last? One day? One week? A month? Fill in 10 points on an Idea Web.

**32. The Five Senses** You can use adjectives to tell how something **looks**, **feels**, **sounds**, **tastes**, or **smells**. For example:

**(looks)**
my **green** sweater

**(feels)**
the **smooth** glass

**(sounds)**
a **buzzing** doorbell

**(tastes)**
the **sour** lemon

**(smells)**
the **strong** cleaning fluid

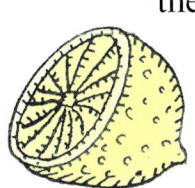

continued on the next page ...

a) Write at least 3 sense words that tell how each of these things might **look**, **feel**, **sound**, **taste**, or **smell**.
1. perfume **smells** …
2. a peach **tastes** … and **feels** …
3. an elephant **looks** … and **sounds** …
4. a bag of popcorn **smells** … and **tastes** …

b) Choose 5 objects. Complete as many columns as you can in this organizer chart:

| Object | Looks | Feels | Sounds | Tastes | Smells |
|--------|-------|-------|--------|--------|--------|
|        |       |       |        |        |        |

33. **Elemenno/LMNO**  Play **Elemenno**. Pick some letters in a row from the alphabet. Choose words that start with those letters to make sentences. Like this:

**B** ackyard
**C** amping
**D** oes
**E** ncourage
**F** riendship

a) Complete these Elemennos:

| **A** ll | **G** oalies | **Q** uiet |
| **B** aseball | **H** ide | **R** ooms |
| **C** ? | **I** ? | **S** ? |
| **D** ? | **J** ? | **T** ? |

b) Create a **Backwards Elemenno** by choosing your letters in backward order.
Do it like this:

**E** very
**D** riveway
**C** ontains
**B** rave
**A** nts

c) Another way to do Elemennos is to use every other letter from the alphabet. Write Elemennos using these rows of letters:

| A | J | K |
| C | L | M |
| E | N | O |
| G | P | Q |

SPELLING STRETCH

140

## 34. Word Trips

**a)** Complete this **word trip**. Copy the boxes and follow the arrows to fill in the spaces. Write a word you think of when you say the word in the box you just left.

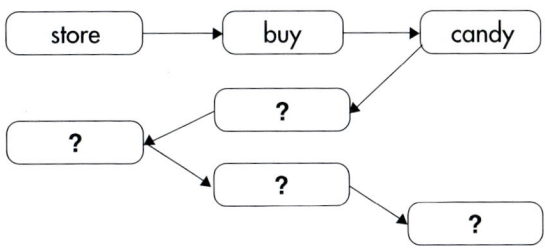

**b)** Make 3 of your own word trips. You may start with these words or choose your own ideas. Make each word trip at least 7 words long.

**music money games**

**c)** Pick a word trip from **b)** and write a story that will illustrate most of the words you wrote.

## 35. E x p a n d Your Word Use

**a)** E x p a n d your stories by using more-descriptive words in your writing! For example, other words that could be used for **run** are:

**chase, scurry, rush, flee, dart**

Can you think of some other **run** words? Try to write 3 more.

**b)** Write at least 3 more-interesting words for each of these often-used words. (**Hint**: You can use the **thesaurus** to find more-descriptive words.)

1 nice  2 cry  3 sad  4 happy  5 fun

**c)** Rewrite these sentences, replacing the words printed in bold with more-interesting ones.
1 The **nice** woman walked **away**.
2 A **big** dog growled at the **scared** children.
3 "We will be **happy** at the beach," **said** Sean.
4 We **laughed** when we **saw** the **sad** circus clown **fall off** the ladder.

**36. Sound Inventions** Some words sound like what they are describing. For example:

**pop** sounds like a balloon bursting

**buzz** sounds like a bee in the flowers

a) Write the following words and beside each write 3 things it could be describing.

| | | | | | |
|---|---|---|---|---|---|
| 1 | crunch | 2 | thump | 3 | squeak |
| 4 | swoosh | 5 | chatter | 6 | howl |
| 7 | crackle | 8 | sizzle | 9 | jingle |
| 10 | flutter | 11 | grunt | 12 | clang |

b) Invent your own sound words. For example:

**flump** could be the sound of a pillow hitting the floor

**ker-splunk** could be the sound of a frog jumping into a pond

Write down each of these things. Make up a word that sounds like the thing.

| | | | | | |
|---|---|---|---|---|---|
| 1 | thunder | 2 | wind | 3 | horse |
| 4 | wet running shoes | 5 | butterfly | 6 | fire |
| 7 | leaf | 8 | chalk | | |

SPELLING STRETCH

# Word List

Words printed in **bold** are **challenge words**.

| **A** | **Lesson** |
|---|---|
| able | 2 |
| action | 15 |
| addition | 15 |
| alphabet | 21 |
| angry | 29 |
| ant | 32 |
| asked | 27 |
| attack | 14 |
| aunt | 32 |
| author | 25 |

**B**
- beak . . . . . . . . 3
- **because** . . . . . 17
- best . . . . . . . . 1
- between . . . . . 3
- birch . . . . . . . 25
- birthday . . . . . 29
- blank . . . . . . . 13
- blink . . . . . . . 13
- brick . . . . . . . 14
- bridge . . . . . . 23
- broken . . . . . . 7
- bunch . . . . . . 16

**C**
- cage . . . . . . . . 2
- canary . . . . . . 19
- cannot . . . . . . 19
- careless . . . . . 28
- castle . . . . . . . 31
- caught . . . . . . 31
- cemetery . . . . 19
- chain . . . . . . . 16
- chance . . . . . . 16
- chapter . . . . . 16
- cherry . . . . . . 16
- child . . . . . . . . 4
- chunk . . . . . . 13
- Churchill . . . . 16
- circus . . . . . . 25
- cities . . . . . . . 19
- climb . . . . . . . 31
- closed . . . . . . 27
- coach . . . . . . . 7
- coast . . . . . . . 19
- collection . . . . 15
- comfortable . . 28
- cone . . . . . . . . 7
- couch . . . . . . 22
- cough . . . . . . 17
- country . . . . . 22
- couple . . . . . . 22
- **course** . . . . . . 17
- cousin . . . . . . 22
- cranky . . . . . . 13
- cried . . . . . . . 27
- curve . . . . . . . 25
- cutting . . . . . . 19

**D**
- dance . . . . . . 19
- daylight . . . . . 20
- dear . . . . . . . . 32
- deep . . . . . . . . 3
- deer . . . . . . . . 32
- delay . . . . . . . 29
- dependable . . 28
- died . . . . . . . . 4
- direction . . . . 15
- dirty . . . . . . . 29
- dock . . . . . . . 14
- donkey . . . . . 29
- doubt . . . . . . 22
- drank . . . . . . 13
- drink . . . . . . . 13
- during . . . . . . 8

**E**
- easy . . . . . . . . 3
- edge . . . . . . . 23
- education . . . . 15
- eight . . . . . . . 20
- elephant . . . . . 21
- endless . . . . . 28
- enemy . . . . . . 1
- enjoy . . . . . . . 1
- enough . . . . . 17
- example . . . . . 26
- except . . . . . . 26
- exercise . . . . . 26
- explosion . . . . 26

**F**
- facts . . . . . . . 1
- **favourite** . . . . 13
- fearless . . . . . 28
- **finally** . . . . . . 13
- **first** . . . . . . . 13
- flew . . . . . . . . 8
- foggy . . . . . . . 1
- French . . . . . . 16
- **friend** . . . . . . 9
- frightened . . . 20
- fruit . . . . . . . . 8

**G**
- gallop . . . . . . 23
- garage . . . . . . 23
- gentle . . . . . . 23
- giant . . . . . . . 23
- glove . . . . . . . 23
- goose . . . . . . 23
- gopher . . . . . . 21
- graph . . . . . . 21
- greatest . . . . . 23
- guess . . . . . . . 23

**H**
- half . . . . . . . . 31
- **heard** . . . . . . 17
- height . . . . . . 20
- hello . . . . . . . 7
- helpless . . . . . 28
- hiding . . . . . . 4
- highway . . . . 20
- hike . . . . . . . . 4
- hockey . . . . . . 14
- hours . . . . . . 22
- huge . . . . . . . 8

**I**
- information . . 15
- instead . . . . . 1
- invention . . . . 15
- it's . . . . . . . . 32
- its . . . . . . . . . 32

**J**
- January . . . . . 29
- July . . . . . . . . 8
- June . . . . . . . 8
- jungle . . . . . . 1

**K**
- key . . . . . . . . 3
- kind . . . . . . . . 4
- kitchen . . . . . 16
- knapsack . . . . 9
- knee . . . . . 3, 31
- knife . . . . . 9, 31

143

knight . . . . . . . . 9
knit . . . . . . . . 9
knob . . . . . . . . 9
knock . . . . . . . . 9
knot . . . . . . . . 9
know . . . . . . . . 9
knowing . . . . . . . . 9
knuckle . . . . . 9

**L**
lamb . . . . . . . . 31
leaves . . . . . . . . 3
life . . . . . . . . 4
listen . . . . . . . . 31
locket . . . . . . . . 14
lovable . . . . . . . . 28
lucky . . . . . . . . 14

**M**
magic . . . . . . . . 19
might . . . . . . . . 4
mighty . . . . . . . . 29
mind . . . . . . . . 4
missed . . . . . . . . 27
month . . . . . . . . 1
motor . . . . . . . . 25

**N**
needed . . . . . . . . 27
nephew . . . . . . . . 21
new . . . . . . . . 8
numb . . . . . . . . 31
nurse . . . . . . . . 25

**O**
owner . . . . . . . . 7

**P**
paid . . . . . . . . 2
painter . . . . . . . . 2
passed . . . . . . . . 32
past . . . . . . . . 32
peace . . . . . . . . 32
peaches . . . . . . . . 16
pharmacy . . . . 21

photograph . . . 21
physical . . . . . 21
picked . . . . . . 27
piece . . . . . . . 32
playground . . . 2
pleased . . . . . . 3
pocket . . . . . . 14
police . . . . . . 19
pollution . . . . 15
position . . . . . 15
post . . . . . . . 7
pray . . . . . . . 29
present . . . . . 26
Prince Edward Island . . . . . . 26
prize . . . . . . . 26
produce . . . . . 26
promise . . . . . 26
proper . . . . . . 26
proud . . . . . . 22
pure . . . . . . . 8
pushed . . . . . . 27

**Q**
quail . . . . . . . 11
quarter . . . . . 11
Quebec . . . . . 11
question . . . . . 11
quick . . . . . . . 11
quickly . . . . . . 11
quiet . . . . . . . 11
quilt . . . . . . . 11

**R**
radio . . . . . . . 2
removable . . . . 28
right . . . . . . 4, 20
rough . . . . . . 17
roughly . . . . . . 17
rowing . . . . . . 7

**S**
scout . . . . . . . 22
secret . . . . . . . 3

shady . . . . . . . 10
shark . . . . . . . 10
shell . . . . . . . 10
shine . . . . . . . 10
shiny . . . . . . . 10
should . . . . . . 10
shout . . . . . . . 22
shower . . . . . . 10
shrank . . . . . . 13
shrink . . . . . . 13
sigh . . . . . . . 20
sight . . . . . . . 20
since . . . . . . . 19
skipped . . . . . . 27
skunk . . . . . . . 13
sly . . . . . . . . 29
smiled . . . . . . 4
smoke . . . . . . 7
sold . . . . . . . 7
sound . . . . . . 22
space . . . . . . . 19
splash . . . . . . 10
square . . . . . . 11
squeeze . . . . . . 11
squirrel . . . . . . 25
stairs . . . . . . . 2
stayed . . . . . . 2
stones . . . . . . 7
stopped . . . . . 27
strange . . . . . . 2
sudden . . . . . . 1
suit . . . . . . . 8
sweep . . . . . . 3

**T**
tail . . . . . . . . 32
tale . . . . . . . . 32
talk . . . . . . . . 31
telephone . . . . 21
**they** . . . . . . . 9
thick . . . . . . . 14
third . . . . . . . 25
threw . . . . . . . 32

through . . . . . . 32
ticket . . . . . . . 14
**told** . . . . . . . 17
tonight . . . . . . 20
tough . . . . . . . 17
track . . . . . . . 14
tried . . . . . . . 27
trinket . . . . . . 13
trophy . . . . . . 21
turtle . . . . . . . 25
twenty . . . . . . 29

**U**
unable . . . . . . 5
uncle . . . . . . . 1
unclean . . . . . . 5
undo . . . . . . . 5
uneven . . . . . . 5
unfair . . . . . . . 5
unhappy . . . . . 5
unlike . . . . . . . 5
unlock . . . . . . 5
unpack . . . . . . 5
untidy . . . . . . 5
untie . . . . . . . 5
use . . . . . . . . 8
useless . . . . . . 28

**V**
vacation . . . . . 15
valuable . . . . . 28

**W**
waited . . . . . . 2
watched . . . . . 16
weigh . . . . . . . 20
**were** . . . . . . . 17
whole . . . . . . . 7
wishes . . . . . . 10
wishful . . . . . . 10
world . . . . . . . 25
wrist . . . . . . . 31
write . . . . . . . 31